# BETTAS, GOURAMIS AND OTHER ANABANTOIDS

## LABYRINTH FISHES OF THE WORLD

DR. JÖRG VIERKE

t.f.h.

Originally published in German by Franckh'sche Verlagshandlung, W. Keller & Co., Stuttgart/1986 under the title *Labyrinthfische: Arten—Haltung—Zucht.*
First edition © 1986 by Franckh'sche Verlagshandlung.

© Copyright 1988 by T.F.H. Publications, Inc. for English translation. A considerable amount of additional new material has been added to the literal German-English translation, including but not limited to additional photographs. Copyright is also claimed for this new material.

**© 1988 by T.F.H. Publications, Inc.**

Distributed in the UNITED STATES by T.F.H. Publications, Inc., One T.F.H. Plaza, Neptune City, NJ 07753; in CANADA to the Pet Trade by H & L Pet Supplies Inc., 27 Kingston Crescent, Kitchener, Ontario N2B 2T6; Rolf C. Hagen Ltd., 3225 Sartelon Street, Montreal 382 Quebec; in CANADA to the Book Trade by Macmillan of Canada (A Division of Canada Publishing Corporation), 164 Commander Boulevard, Agincourt, Ontario M1S 3C7; in ENGLAND by T.F.H. Publications Limited, Cliveden House/Priors Way/Bray, Maidenhead, Berkshire SL6 2HP, England; in AUSTRALIA AND THE SOUTH PACIFIC by T.F.H. (Australia) Pty. Ltd., Box 149, Brookvale 2100 N.S.W., Australia; in NEW ZEALAND by Ross Haines & Son, Ltd., 18 Monmouth Street, Grey Lynn, Auckland 2, New Zealand; in SINGAPORE AND MALAYSIA by MPH Distributors (S) Pte., Ltd., 601 Sims Drive, #03/07/21, Singapore 1438; in the PHILIPPINES by Bio-Research, 5 Lippay Street, San Lorenzo Village, Makati Rizal; in SOUTH AFRICA by Multipet Pty. Ltd., 30 Turners Avenue, Durban 4001. Published by T.F.H. Publications, Inc. Manufactured in the United States of America by T.F.H. Publications, Inc.

# CONTENTS

Standing waters like this beautiful pond in southern Thailand often contain labyrinth fishes. This specific pond actually contained Siamese Fighting Fish, *Betta splendens*, and Croaking Gourami (*Trichopsis vittatus*). Photo by the author.

# Preface

Labyrinth fishes, the often splendidly colored yet unpretentious exotics that conquered the hearts of aquarists 100 years ago, are enjoying a comeback. Never before have so many new bettas, gouramis, and other labyrinths been imported as in the last ten years. Many are new for the hobbyist, and many are new to science. The reason for that is mainly the extensive travel of a few dedicated aquarists who did not mind the effort and cost involved in searching for rare and unknown fishes in their own native habitats. Thanks to that effort and expense, our knowledge of the distribution and behavior of these fishes has grown along with our understanding of how to keep and breed them. There are, naturally, besides the many unpretentious and attractive aquarium fishes, other kinds which are among the hardcore problem fishes, fishes which aquarists have never been able to breed. There is still much to be discovered.

I, myself, have made several trips to the native habitats of the labyrinth fishes, as well as engaged in several scientific studies of them. Without the ample help of friends and acquaintances, however, I would have only been able to do a fraction of the work represented here. Many helped me to obtain rare living specimens; others made preserved specimens available for study; and still others helped me with the literature or in other ways. I can only name a few of the many friends here who have helped me and whom I want to thank: B. and A. Brown (Unsworth), Dr. W. Foersch (Munich), Heah, S. H. (Kuala Lumpur), M. Kottelat (Basel), S. Liebetrau (Kennewick), O. Naujokat (Remscheid), Dr. T. Roberts (San Francisco), D. Schaller (Munich), H. Scheuermann (Berlin), and Dato Sharum Bin Yub (Kuala Lumpur). To these and others I express my appreciation that this book is so comprehensive and up to date. May it inspire and help the labyrinth enthusiasts in their interesting and entertaining hours at the aquarium.

*Dr. Jorg Vierke*

# Labyrinth Fishes and Their Characteristics

The most characteristic thing about a labyrinth fish is an air-filled breathing cavity, the labyrinth, located above the gills under the operculum or gill cover. This cavity supplements the breathing function of the gills and can be compared functionally to lungs. It is lined with well vascularized tissue and is well suited to gaseous interchange. The fish rises regularly to the surface and exchanges used air for fresh air. This accessory breathing makes it possible for labyrinth fishes to survive even in waters with very little oxygen content. Under natural conditions, most labyrinth fishes depend upon labyrinth breathing. If they are experimentally deprived of their air-breathing capability, they suffocate. Only in oxygen-saturated water—which scarcely occurs in nature—do their gills

The labyrinth organ of an African climbing perch. The gill cover is cut away to show the first gill arch (C), the gills (B), and the complex labyrinth organ (A). Drawn by the author.

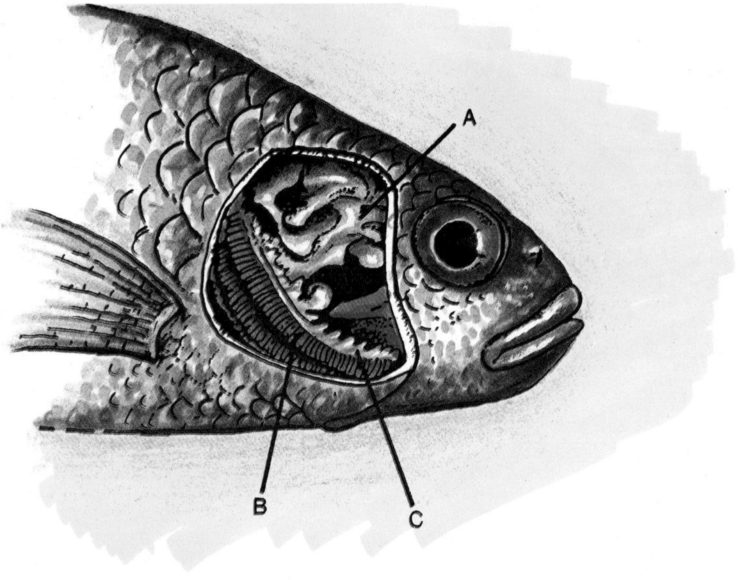

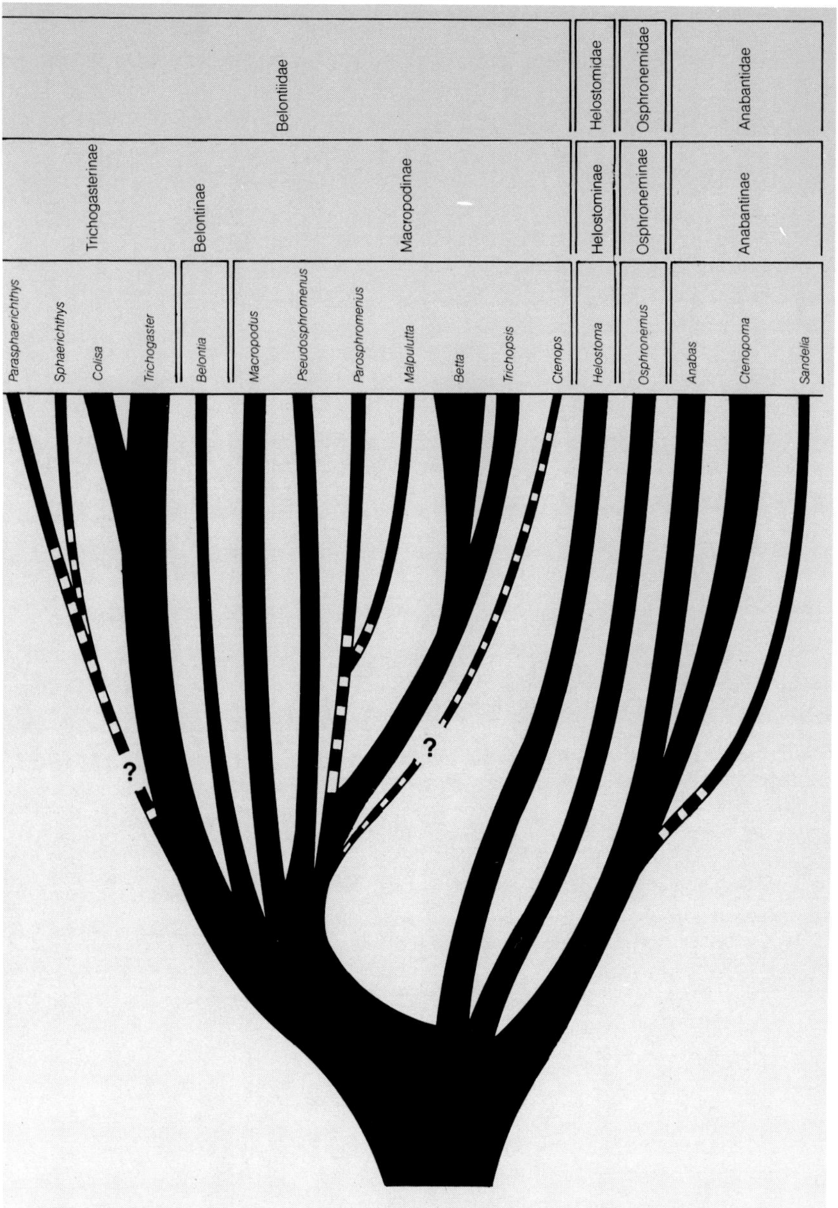


This genealogical tree presents the relationship of the anabantoids' genera. It is based upon the typical characteristics by which ichthyologists classify all fishes, namely body proportions and meristics. The dotted lines indicate uncertainty. Since definitive works on this group are still awaited, conclusions must be carefully drawn from this tree. The further breakdown of the subfamilies Trichogasterinae or Macropodinae would be premature. Drawing by J. Dittmar based upon direction from the author.

suffice. (There are exceptions to this. For instance, under normal conditions the little gouramis, *Parosphromenus*, hardly resort at all to labyrinth breathing.)

The labyrinth cavity can be confused with the inner ear—also called a labyrinth—which fish and all other vertebrates, including man, have. That is understandable because both organs are located at about the same place in the head. Beyond that, however, the ear's labyrinth and the labyrinth organ do not have anything in common.

In addition to the true labyrinth fishes, fishes of the gen ra *Channa* (snakeheads) and *Clarias* (gill-sack catfish) and a few others also possess a respiratory labyrinth. These fishes are sometimes kept in aquaria, but we won't discuss them here. All the fishes considered here belong to the order Perciformes, forming their own suborder of about 80 species, the true labyrinth, anabantoid, or climbing perches (Anabantoidei). The name *climbing perch* comes from one of the best-known representatives of this suborder, the climbing perch, *Anabas*, a common food fish in all southern and southeastern Asia. It is known for climbing out of its native waters and migrating to new habitats.

All anabantoids are tropical and subtropical freshwater fishes that are very rarely found in brackish water. They are usually moderately elongated fishes with a single spinous dorsal fin and anteriorly inserted pelvic (ventral) fins. The caudal fin is often long, and the anal opening lies in the anterior half of the body, often even the anterior third. All species are egg-layers, and most care for their broods. A few of the Asiatic species are mouthbrooders, but many build bubblenests.

Taxonomists usually classify the labyrinth fishes as follows:

Family **ANABANTIDAE**
(Genera: *Anabas*, *Ctenopoma*, *Sandelia*)

Family **BELONTIIDAE**
(Genera: *Belontia*, *Betta*, *Colisa*, *Ctenops*, *Helostoma*, *Malpulutta*, *Parosphromenus*, *Pseudosphromenus*, *Sphaerichthys*, *Trichogaster*, *Trichopsis*)

Family **OSPHRONEMIDAE**
(Genus *Osphronemus*)

Family **HELOSTOMATIDAE**
(Genus *Helostoma*)

The genealogical tree presents the relationship of the genera in greater detail. It was based primarily upon bony structure (Liem) and behavior (Vierke). Dotted lines indicate uncertainty. To deduce, for example, a further breakdown of the subfamilies Trichogasterinae or Macropodinae, would certainly be premature.

# Habitat and Distribution

The home of the labyrinth fishes is primarily in tropical Africa and Asia. Only in a few places, such as southern Africa and eastern Asia do they extend into subtropical areas.

Rice paddies are the preferred habitat of many labyrinth fishes in Southeast Asia. Along with the gouramis and climbing perches, there are also snakeheads, *Channa*, *Rasbora* species, catfishes, and snakes. Photo by the author.

Their special adaptation, the labyrinth organ, characterizes them as animals that at least periodically occur in oxygen-poor marshes and swampy regions. Such habitats are typical mostly in coastal rain-forest areas from which water runs off very slowly at certain times, leaving the rain forest and other habitats flooded for long periods. Many species adapted to these natural swamps have been able to move into and populate man-made swamps, the rice paddies of tropical Asia. These immigrant fishes include, besides important food fishes like the climbing perch (*Anabas*), the kissing gourami, and the snake-skin gourami, many favorite aquarium fishes such as *Colisa* species and *Betta splendens*, the Siamese fighting fish.

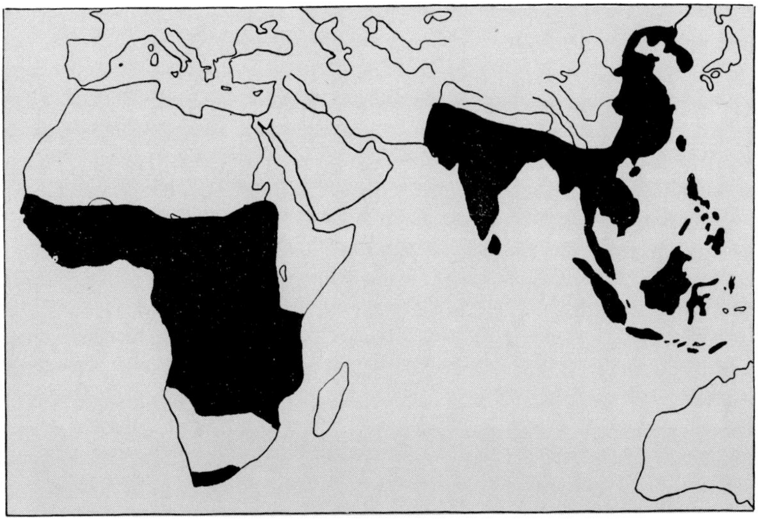

The natural distribution of the labyrinth fishes. This is interesting because there are no labyrinth fishes in North or South America even though these continents were once united with Africa. Drawing by the author.

Labyrinth fishes occur in often quite precarious habitats in which the only other fishes that can exist are those also equipped with accessory respiratory organs (snakeheads, clariid catfishes, and bichirs), places such as wells, water-filled wagon ruts and cattle trails, and even sewage canals. So, it's no wonder that many labyrinth fishes are among the most hardy fishes in aquaria.

Even if the labyrinth fishes were indeed originally swamp-dwellers that adapted to often high temperatures and extremely oxygen-poor stagnating standing water, there are nevertheless many species today that populate other habitats. They live in the cooler flowing waters of tropical rain forests and also require similar conditions in the aquarium. Really fast-moving waters, however, have been populated by

*Betta splendens*, the Siamese Fighting Fish, is one of the many adaptable fishes belonging to the labyrinth group which have been able to move into many man-made environments (like rice paddies) and survive. Historically, fishes which have been unable to adapt to changing environments become extinct.

only a few species. At any rate, all labyrinth fishes have remained tropical inhabitants of the flat lands near coasts and large rivers.

The actual distribution of only a few species has been studied. This is not surprising when you realize how extensive the regions concerned are and that great expanses consist only of inaccessible wilderness.

Economically important fishes among the labyrinths (particularly *Anabas*, *Osphronemus*, *Helostoma*, and *Trichogaster pectoralis*) have been introduced by man to extensive areas of southern and southeastern Asia. This "naturalization" has made it, in part, impossible to determine the original homelands of these fishes. There is no doubt that the labyrinth fishes originated in Asia. We may picture their not quite labyrinth-breathing ancestors as looking somewhat like today's dwarf chameleon fish (*Badis*). *Badis* are related quite closely to

the labyrinth fishes, and even their breeding behavior reminds us of the labyrinths.

Following the development of labyrinth-breathing ancestors, several more forms developed in southern and southeastern Asia. These became the ancestors of the current subfamilies. This occurred about 40 or 50 million years ago. But how did the labyrinth fishes first get to Africa?

The African labyrinth genera *Ctenopoma* and *Sandelia* are doubtlessly closely related to the Asiatic genus *Anabas* and are, therefore, included together with the family Anabantidae. It cannot have been too long—geologically speaking, of course—since the members of this family still had a common ancestor; it was probably "only" 25 to 20 million years ago. At that time Africa was connected with Asia via a broad, climatically favorable land bridge that facilitated a progressive westward migration of many animals, including fishes. Today these same landscapes (Arabia, Iran) are predominantly desert.

With *Sandelia* and *Ctenopoma* species we are possibly dealing with the descendants of two or perhaps several separate migratory waves. This is known to have occurred with other species. I don't agree with the far-fetched idea that *Anabas* came to Asia from Africa during the earth's geologic middle ages via the northward drifting of the Indian subcontinent as part of the overall continental drift.

# Behavior and Ecology

There is no fish group that can approach the labyrinth fishes when it comes to the multiplicity of interesting behavior. Even the favorite subjects of behavioral researchers, the cichlids, fall short in comparison with the labyrinth fishes. The labyrinth fishes include fishes that can leave their natural habitat—water—and travel overland. They include fishes that can spit out well-aimed water droplets to knock their prey into the water. The anabantoids also include the kissing gouramis, fish that fight most impressively with their mouth. They also include fishes that survive the dry season by burying themselves in dried up river and pond beds. Included also are fishes that sleep on the ground during the day and others that can make louder noises than any other aquarium fishes. In addition, there are very different and often highly distinctive reproductive habits that vary from species to species. There are non-brooding labyrinth fishes, bubblenest builders, cave or hole brooders, and mouthbrooders. Most of these behavioral aspects can be observed in your own living room. This is a good reason, besides their often attractive coloration, for their continually increasing popularity among hobbyists.

## Adaptations to Annual Dry Periods

Only a few labyrinth fishes live in largely uniform and stable jungle habitats. Most species are adapted to the annual dry and rainy seasons. When the waters progressively evaporate during the dry period, the fishes that do not save themselves by going into deeper bodies of water or rivers perish when their habitat is fully dried up.

A few labyrinth fishes, however, are able to bury themselves in the bottom of dried up puddles and swamps. They can survive through long periods of dryness in moist cavities in the hardened bottom. When the water again fills the depression or other parched basin during the rainy period, the bottom softens and the fish come out again. This art of survival is practiced in Africa by the spiny *Ctenopoma multispinis* and by both of the Asian climbing perch species (*Anabas*), as well as by *Betta splendens* and perhaps also by the closely related species *B. smaragdina* and B. imbellis.

*Betta splendens* can survive even if thick, clay mud is all that's left of the water. In the hard clay and mud, you can find holes about a finger's thickness, and down in the lower end of each hole is a thick (ant proof!) mud plug. Behind that plug is a rolled-up fighting fish, which immediately becomes active if you transfer it to clear water. The fighting fish, however, do not survive total drying out of the bottom.

The climbing perch *Anabas* can bury itself even deeper. It doesn't bother the fish if the bottoms of once-wet ponds and puddles become hard as stone and bone dry. During the dry season the natives can't get to this fish, which is one of their foods. It's been assumed that the climbing perch burrow down to the groundwater when the surface waters dry up. As soon as the ponds and rice fields fill up again after the heavy rains, the fish reappear.

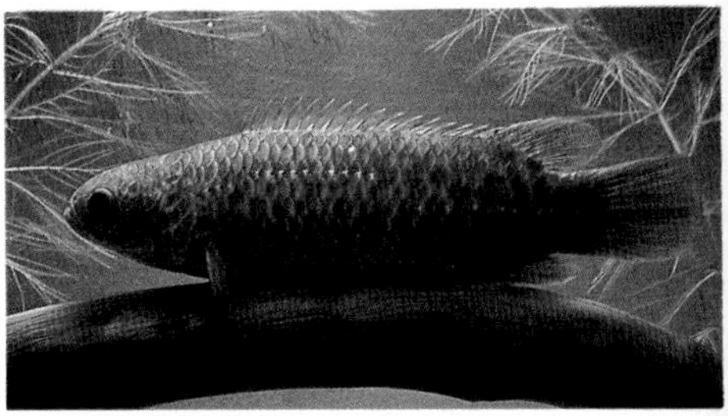

*Ctenopoma multispinis* can survive during dry periods in the hardened bottom of a dried-up lake bed. Photo by Dr. W. Foersch.

*Anabas* and *Ctenopoma multispinis* are, in addition, able to leave their puddles and travel overland in the search for new water in which to live. Movement along the ground is by means of wriggling; the spines of the ventral fins and the powerful spines of the spread-out gill covers also help by anchoring, providing them with a foothold. With backward flexing and stretching, these fishes can snake along astonishingly fast. The Asian climbing perches usually move along overland in their normal body position, while *Ctenopoma multispinis* gets along on its side—tail flicks drive the fish along in little jumps during which the serrated margin of the widely

This fish out of water does very well in "walking." The climbing perch, *Anabas testudineus*, has the ability to move over land from one pool to another and thereby leave polluted or desiccating small bodies of water. During their journeys, they often fall prey to snakes, birds, mammals and other predatory creatures, including man. Photo by the author.

opened gill cover lends a foothold against which to push. The giant fighting fish, *Betta unimaculata*, has also been reported to migrate overland.

Many labyrinth fishes swim in rivers at the start of the rainy season and form into more or less large schools. They are rather colorless then and very cautious, often settling down very still at the bottom. To get air, the whole school rushes to the surface and then dives down out of sight. We can occasionally observe this schooling behavior in the aquarium, too, mainly with *Colisa* and *Trichogaster* species when a large number are kept together.

When the rivers overflow their banks at the beginning of the rainy season and flood the low-lying land, the labyrinth fishes disperse in the rapidly warming water and seek tranquil places that appear suitable for establishing their breeding territories. Then the males build nests and the fish breed and raise their broods.

## Feeding Behavior

The labyrinth fishes include species (like some fighting fishes) that go after relatively large prey, as well as rather harmless filter-feeders (such as the kissing gourami). Only a few species like plant food, including the edible giant gourami (*Osphronemus*) and the climbing perch (*Anabas*).

Most labyrinth fishes are carnivorous by nature. Among them, *Colisa* and *Trichogaster* have the most varied possibilities of feeding. Five different methods can be observed:

1) *Snapping*. This is the usual method, as you can see in the aquarium. A morsel of food or prey is quickly aimed at, snapped up, possibly chewed, and then swallowed.

2) *Scooping/Gulping*. The fish goes to the surface and sucks in everything floating on the surface. The gill covers act as a suction pump. In the aquarium, food consists mainly of tiny fragments of dry food; in the wild, it's pollen and other small particles.

3) *Grazing*. This is a method used by kissing gouramis as well as by "thread-finned" gouramis. They constantly work over algae-coated plants and other objects with their mouth without, however, any visible effect on the algal crop. Grazing appears to be directed at the microscopic animals living in the algae.

4) *Jumping*. Tame labyrinth fishes also try to catch food by jumping if you hold a tidbit an inch or so above the water surface of their aquarium. We don't know yet what the significance of this behavior is in the wild state.

This *Colisa sota* is demonstrating the snapping behavior during feeding. The glass larvae it is eating is reputed to choke some small anabantoids. Photos by Hans-Joachim Richter.

5) *Spitting*. Not the most frequent but certainly the most interesting method of feeding is by spitting water at food and prey

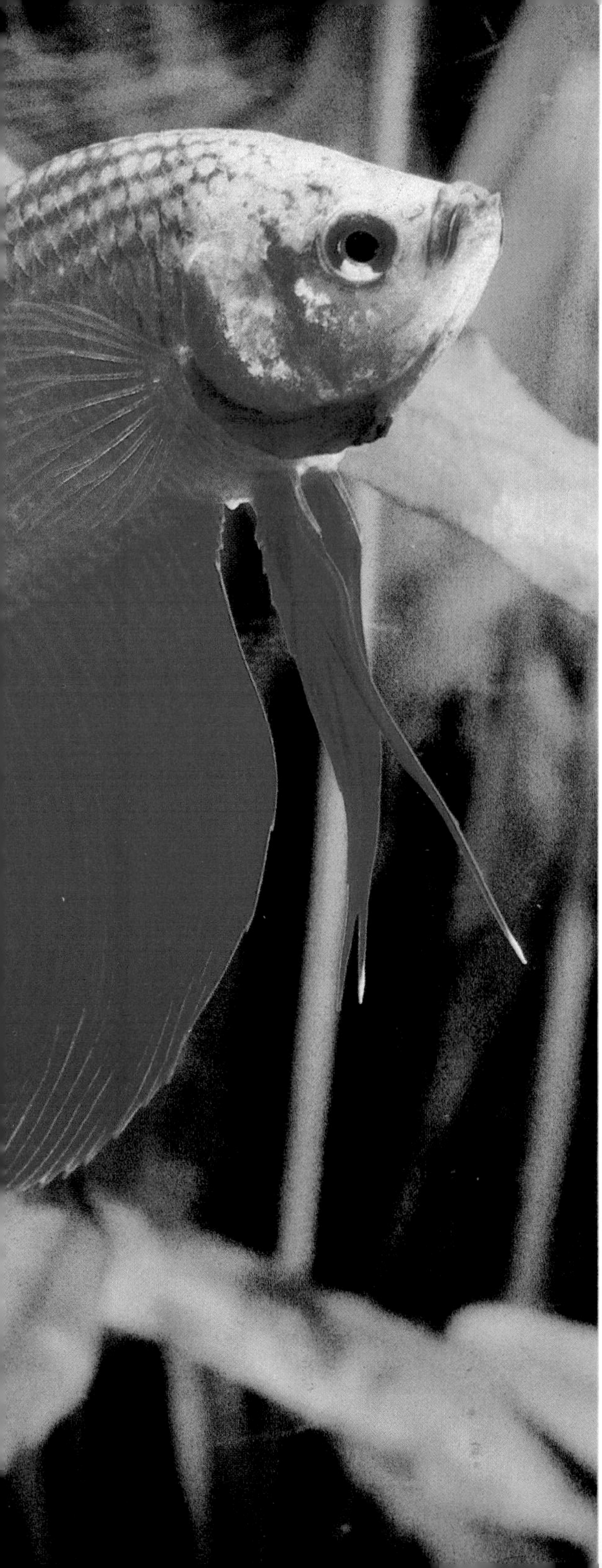

*Betta splendens* Photo By
H. J. Richter

A blue gourami, *Trichogaster trichopterus*, spitting at a small fly. It hopes to knock the prey into the water where it quickly snaps it up. Photo by Ruda Zukal.

located *out of* the water. The objects struck by the waterdrop are knocked into the water and eaten.

To catch prey by spitting, the fish come to the surface, aim, and then pelt the target with a rapid sequence of water droplets. A salvo can consist of up to 13 droplets in intervals of 1/8 to 1/20 second. Every droplet is projected out of the mouth by closure of the gill covers. Opening the gill covers aspirates a new supply of water through the gills. Normally, spitting consists of four to eight single drops and lasts only half a second.

Water spitting is seen mainly in threadfins, especially the dwarf gourami, *Colisa lalia*. Unfortunately, it doesn't demonstrate this interesting behavior very often in the aquarium. We still are not certain about the food-gathering significance of this behavior in the wild state.

## Fighting Behavior

Aggression in fishes can easily become a problem for aquarists. Males are especially pugnacious during the breeding period. At other times, however, labyrinth fishes get along together and with other kinds of fishes, except perhaps for harmless little quarrels when feeding or establishing hierarchy (rank order) among themselves. Fighting to establish social ranking occurs in all aquaria, especially among closely related fishes, for whom it is important to once and for all determine which has priority at the feeding spot or in the aquarium. The most violent fighting about social ranking usually occurs among fish of the same species, mainly among those of the same sex. Once it has been made clear just which is the stronger fish, there is usually peace for a long while.

Labyrinth fishes that are ready to breed are particularly aggressive. That applies above all to the territorial species, particularly the males. As a rule,

Two male Siamese Fighting Fish, *Betta splendens*, engaged in combat. The fish tear at each other's fins until they are shredded. Rarely does the fish which loses the battle perish from wounds. They may, however, develop bacterial or fungus infections. Photo by Gene Wolfsheimer.

they build bubblenests from whose surroundings they energetically chase all intruders. The females which are tolerated for only a short time under the nest just for spawning, also are vigorously chased away. The enclosed conditions of the aquarium, which rob the female of a hiding place or room to escape, have turned many males into unwitting murderers of their spouses.

The fighting of breeding males for the possession and setting the limits of their territory begins with threats that escalate, through several steps, to actual fighting. The fight itself is vigorous and can lead to losses, although the biological purpose of the pre-combat rituals is to avoid those losses. The weaker opponent is warned and has the chance to make a timely retreat, at least in the wild state.

The first step in threatening is to impress. They first attempt to make themselves seem as large as possible by spreading their fins and gill covers. In the broadside display, the threatening fish—with fins spread under full tension—places himself across his opponent's path. This posture is called the T-position.

Fishes such as *Betta splendens, Macropodus opercularis*, and various climbing perches that can spread their gill covers, also threaten head on. The opponent, with his spread gill covers, appears to be two or three times his real size, especially

Battling Siamese Fighting Fish is enjoyed as a sport in Thailand (Siam). The fish fight until one of them gives up. Photo by Gene Wolfsheimer.

when spots on the gill cover margins (as in *Macropodus*) look like widely separated eyes. Frontal threatening, however, is also observed in fishes that do not spread their gill covers.

Two male Siamese Fighting Fish approach each other with extended gill covers in a head-on threat. Retouched photo by W.T.Innes.

Another stage in the threatening process consists in sending a pressure wave against one another by undulating body movements or beating with the tail fin. The intensity of the pressure waves can be perceived quite well by the opponent on his lateral line and will give him an idea of the strength of his antagonist. In this stage the fish are positioned parallel to one another, either head to head or head to tail (inversely parallel).

The inversely parallel position often changes into a typical merry-go-round swim, each fish trying to bite his opponent on the tail. This can become quite violent and often decides the outcome of the fight. Frequently the victor chases the vanquished for a while and bites him.

The head-on threat is usually carried along further in mouth-fighting. The methods vary greatly

This male Siamese Fighting Fish is approaching a female of the same species in the typical battle fashion of fighting males.

from species to species. In the case of the kissing gourami and "thread-finned" gouramis, these fights often seem harmless and are often misunderstood by observers, who think the fish are kissing. The contenders swim calmly toward each other, mouths gaping, and bite one another for short periods; no shoving or pulling occurs. Then they back off to their initial places but soon come in to bite again. If one of the combatants rises to the surface of the water to breathe, his opponent doesn't take the opportunity to attack, but generally also uses the time to catch his own breath.

The mouth-fights of *Macropodus*, *Belontia*, and others, are more dramatic. They seize one another on the mouth and hold on for minutes. In this way they keep their opponents from breathing, thus finding out who is the stronger.

The fighting of the croaking gourami (*Trichopsis vittatus*) is particularly interesting. They

threaten one another head-on, at first with gaping and projected snout. Then they slowly roll over on their side and arch themselves. Next they strike lightning fast, bite each other on the snout for about half a second, and break apart again. In this phase the croaking gourami doesn't make a sound, but it vocalizes strongly during threat behavior. This "vocalization" sounds more like a baby rattle than croaking or growling and is accompanied by rapid fanning of the pectoral fins. The growling is produced by the pectoral fin musculature, whose strongly developed upper fibers glide over parts of the skeleton. The labyrinth cavity serves as a resonating chamber that amplifies the sound.

Males of the *Colisa* species (except *Colisa sota*) also can produce clearly audible sounds. That occurs mostly when defending the brood. At that time the brood-watching males quickly dash out of their nests at intruders. In these thrusting attacks growling sounds are clearly audible and usually give the intruders a chance to still get out of the danger zone just as fast as possible. The warning sounds are apparently made by vibrations in the air-filled labyrinth cavities, because you can see a small burst of air bubbles escape from the gill covers whenever the sounds are made.

## Reproductive Behavior

All labyrinth fishes release sperm and eggs into the open water rather than onto a substrate or base. A few species leave their eggs to their own fate at this point. Others, the brooders, take care of their eggs and hatchlings. Only the Siamese fighting fish (*Betta splendens*) is known to be actively concerned for its free-swimming young.

For actual mating, the anabantoid male embraces (wraps himself around) the female in various ways. The wrapping around behavior guarantees timely discharge of the sexual products and at the same time keeps the eggs and sperm as close together as possible, since the genital openings of both parents are brought close together by this maneuver. That is important because the sperm cells don't live long in water and have to fertilize the egg within a minute.

In non-brooding species, for example in many climbing perches, the males pursue the females for quite a while. Finally, the female hesitates a moment, and the male seizes her for the few seconds the embrace requires. The eggs float under the surface of the water and can be carried along by wind and current. Significantly, non-brooders spawn only in calm, non-flowing waters. The spawn of the kissing gourami (*Helostoma*) is exceptional in that it is sticky and adheres to aquatic plants.

In brooding labyrinth fishes, the male's readiness to spawn is expressed in his territorial behavior. Every fish, above all those of the same species, is chased out of the territory. A bubblenest is built somewhere in

SPAWNING METHODS OF BUBBLENEST BUILDERS: Usually the male builds a floating nest of bubbles. Figure 1 shows a male Siamese Fighter preparing his nest. In figure 2, the male mates with the female and squeezes the eggs out of her. This same behavior is also shown in figure 3, but this time it is *Trichopsis vittatus*! Photos by the author.

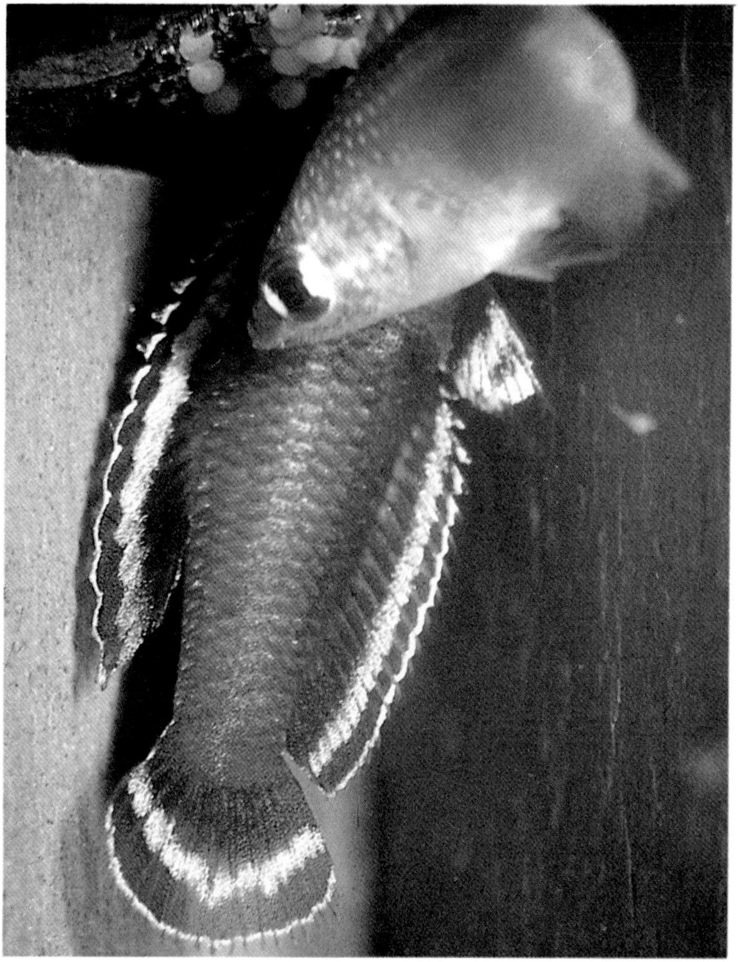

the territory. Some fish build it in holes near the bottom or under horizontally disposed leaves, and some build it right at the surface of the water. The majority of these species, however, set their nests in the open on aquatic and swamp plants that project over the water.

*Parosphromenus nagyi* spawning. Note the very large eggs. The fish spawn in a cave, usually laying their eggs in a very secretive spawning ritual. Photo by the author.

The nest is often constructed on floating aquatic plants in such a way that it appears to be made of vegetable matter, but only two thread-finned species (*Colisa lalia* and *Trichogaster microlepis*) and the edible gourami (*Osphronemus goramy*) actively gather vegetable matter for use in their nests.

The dwarf thread-finned male *Colisa lalia* often spits plant matter (blades, fibers, grass fragments, etc.) into the foam of his nest at the surface of the water so forcibly that bits and pieces of vegetation shoot up out of the water. In this way the construction material is often well anchored on the plants that stick up out of the water, thus reducing the chances of the floating nest drifting away. In aquaria the nest can even wind up on the cover of the tank.

Once the male has completed the nest, he attempts to entice the female under it with characteristic courtship signals and "leading" or directional swimming. At first you can hardly tell whether it's courtship or fighting, because the threat posturing is confusingly similar in both cases.

The embrace can occur in

*Colisa fasciata* male building his bubblenest. Photo by the author.

various ways, according to species. Among the thread-finned gouramis, the male positions himself across the path of the female and he is approached broadside. When his side is touched, the embrace reaction is triggered, and he bends himself around the female.

Among the croaking gouramis (*Trichopsis* spp.), it's exactly the opposite. In these species the male swims into the broad side of the female. In other genera there are transitional forms between these two extremes, such as with *Pseudosphromenus*, in which both

Two types of spawning embraces. Below is *Betta unimaculata* which embraces on the bottom; to the right is *Betta splendens* which spawns high in the water under its bubblenest. Photos by the author.

fish mutually embrace.

As for spawning behavior of the labyrinth fishes, various concepts are used here. The pre-spawning phase often lasts for hours, followed by pseudo-spawning and then spawning. *False-spawning* is spawning behavior, but without release of the eggs. *Pseudo-spawning* occurs either at the beginning or at the end of spawning. *Spawning* is the single embrace culminating in release of the eggs. Subsequently, either both parents or just one of them brings the eggs to the nest.

There are several basic differences between non-brooders and brooders that developed independently in response to local conditions. The similar characteristics and behavior in these cases do not have anything

to do with relationships, and thus should only be used for taxonomic studies after very careful consideration in every instance. That is especially true for climbing perches.

In addition to the many African climbing perches, *Anabas* and *Helostoma* also belong to the non-brooders. It's interesting that, in contrast to most brooding labyrinth fishes (except *Trichopsis pumilus* and *Colisa sota*), the females of many (or all?) non-brooders are larger than the males. That is definitely true in the cases of *Ctenopoma muriei*, *Ctenopoma petherici*, *Ctenopoma kingsleyae*, and *Anabas testudineus*. This sexual dimorphism makes it possible to lay a greater number of eggs, which is necessary for non-brooders.

Moreover, all non-brooding labyrinth fishes are very modestly colored. They live preferably in open, uncluttered waters where, on one hand, they need their camouflage, and, on the other hand, have little opportunity to visually delimit their territories. No territories are founded, and even at breeding time the fishes prefer living in schools or small groups.

*Colisa lalia*, the Dwarf Gourami, in a spawning embrace under its bubblenest. This variety is the domestic golden variety. Photo by the author.

*Macropodus opercularis*, the Paradise Fish, in a spawning embrace under its floating bubblenest. Photo by the author.

Non-brooders spawn mostly in the evening hours or at night. That's why color patterns that serve for courtship are neither rational nor necessary for these fish. They apparently communicate by means of pheromones (attractants released into the water). Observations of *Ctenopoma muriei* at least allow the assumption that sexually mature females release sexually specific substances (to which males react) from their genital papillae. It's naturally quite favorable for night-spawners to live in schools, which obviates the wasteful search for a mate. Spawning at night or during late evening hours is advantageous for non-brooders because it gives

them some headway against the incursions of spawn predators.

Brooders normally build bubblenests that mainly serve to hold eggs and hatchlings. Mating must occur near the nest, ideally directly under it. For this, complex communication mechanisms are required; the male has to present himself and the location of the nest, so he generally shows a characteristic coloration and carries out leading or directional swimming in order to show the female the way to the nest. Such behavior requires that nest-builders mate during the day; they communicate chiefly with visual signals. In addition, nest-builders usually stay in areas along the banks where they can define their territory and anchor their nests to the vegetation, which keeps the nests from being carried away by the water. Brooders, with their compact, usually laterally

(Above): *Trichopsis vittatus* in a spawning embrace in mid-water. The fish to the left are wild-colored Dwarf Gouramis, *Colisa lalia,* in a spawning embrace. *Colisa lalia* normally spawn directly under the bubblenest. Photos by the author.

compressed body form, are more adapted to movement within the narrow confines of aquatic vegetation than are the much faster, torpedo-shaped non-brooders (except *Helostoma*).

Nest-building brooders normally form a patriarchal family; that is, only the male takes care of nest-building, territorial defense, and care of the young. In many species males are set off from the females, especially during courtship, by their brighter colors.

If you look closely at the eggs of brooders, you'll see that they differ according to the species and range from completely transparent (*Colisa*, *Trichogaster*), weakly turbid (*Macropodus*, *Belontia*), milky (*Malpulutta*, *Parosphromenus*), and finally to completely opaque white (*Betta*, *Trichopsis*). The clear eggs are lighter than water and float upward by themselves, right into the bubblenest if mating takes place directly underneath it. The male exclusively takes care of the brood (patriarchy) with this form of nesting.

The milky, turbid, and opaque eggs, on the other hand, are heavier than water, so they sink immediately to the bottom. With this form, both parents must help in caring for the eggs. During the one or more hours of the spawning phase, both parents—unlike typical floating egg producers—stay under the nest. They gather up the eggs that rain down after mating, pick them up from the bottom, and place them in the nest. In so doing, they coat the eggs with a salivary secretion to make them adhere to the froth bubbles of the nest, which are made of the same secretion.

The females of the species that produce sinking eggs also can produce the secretion for nest-building, although they normally don't build them. At times, however, they can indeed be seen constructing nests. After the usual spawning phase when the females are chased away from the vicinity of the nest, they may take some of the spawn with them and care for it "within their own domain" elsewhere, but they usually are satisfied with indirect participation. They stay in an outer defense zone and defend the male's territory from possible intruders; they also remain available to take over brood care if something should happen to the male. This has been observed for *Pseudosphromenus* and *Trichopsis* species and for *Betta splendens*. You can see the same also in the genus *Macropodus*, which, with their slightly turbid floating eggs, take a middle position between typical producers of floating eggs and producers of sinking eggs.

The fry of the producers of sinking eggs are, like the eggs, heavier than water, so they are in constant danger of falling out of their nest. However, they possess organs of attachment on their heads that can adhere to the vegetation, the frothy bubbles of the nest, or even to one another. Yet the young often fall to the bottom anyway, keeping their parents constantly busy. Here, too, is where the supplemental help given by the mother in defending the territory comes in handy.

The more intensive the parents' care of the brood, the greater the chances are of the young growing up. For the preservation of the species, fewer eggs are necessary for the very successful brooders compared to the fishes

(Right): The most famous photograph showing the first recorded spawning of the Chocolate Gourami, *Sphaerichthys osphromenoides*. Photo by Hans-Joachim Richter.

*Colisa sota* pair spawning under their bubblenest. Photo by the author.

that simply disperse their spawn right into the water and take no further care of it. The small number of eggs means that the eggs of the intensive brooders can be larger than those of other fishes. That is advantageous even if the eggs take somewhat longer to develop, because the young fish are already relatively large when they take off on their own and thus skip a dangerous time of life.

Phylogenetically, the non-brooding labyrinth fishes are doubtless the original types. They produce a large number of relatively small eggs. The risks that jeopardize a single spawning are greatly reduced by bubblenests and the associated brooding behavior. A further intensification of brooding occurs among the producers of sinking eggs, particularly so among the mouthbrooders.

Even bubblenest-building and floating eggs, however, are carried phylogenetically to even more intensive and more successful forms of brooding, interestingly, by regression of the bubblenest-building. This occurred three times, independently each time, for the honey gourami, *Colisa sota*; the roundtailed paradisefish, *Macropodus chinensis*; and *Belontia* spp.

The honey gourami, *Colisa sota*, builds a bubblenest at first, often an especially flat one, but lets it fall apart right after spawning. They collect their eggs (often with a trick: water spitting) and gather them into a clump. The

SPAWNING THE SIAMESE FIGHTING FISH: 1. Male attracts willing female. 2. He then builds a bubblenest in earnest. 3. He entices the female under the bubblenest. 4. He embraces her and squeezes heavier-than-water eggs from her. 5. He gathers the eggs in his mouth and spits them into his nest. 6. The fry hatch in a time dependent on the water temperature. 7. A strong light directed at one corner of the nursery tank attracts both the fry and food, especially when *Artemia* nauplii are used. 8. The fry eating newly hatched *Artemia* nauplii. Drawings by John R. Quinn.

1

5

2

6
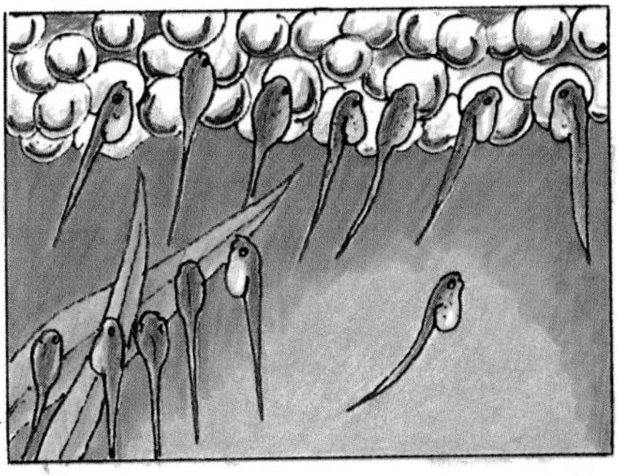

3

7

4

8

1

2

SPAWNING OF *BETTA MACROSTOMA*: The fish spawn in the usual *Betta* manner with the male embracing the female. But the female keeps the eggs in her mouth and hides. The male finds her (1) and the female spits the eggs into his mouth (2). This continues several times during the course of spawning. Sometimes the female still has eggs but the male refuses to take them into his mouth (3 facing page), and avoids a head-on encounter with the female. Photos by Dr. Herbert R. Axelrod.

spittle-held eggs stick together and can be stored in piles just about the size of cherries, very much more unobtrusive than in a bubblenest. Yet the male is forced to stand constant guard over the eggs so the young don't suffocate for lack of oxygen. Direct evidence that this type of brood care is more successful than with other *Colisa* species is the fact that *Colisa sota* produces fewer but larger eggs.

Laying of eggs in compact heaps, in fact, lets the Ceylonese paradisefish carry its brood to safety when danger threatens. When I startled a combtail, *Belontia signata*, male with a photographic flash, he snapped up his whole brood and swam with it to a hiding spot behind a stone at the bottom of the tank. It took several minutes before he came back and replaced the spawn where it had been. The same thing happened with a *Betta splendens* male.

Mouthbrooding is occasionally evident in *Betta splendens* and *Belontia signata*. Actual mouthbrooders are found in the genera *Betta*, *Sphaerichthys*, presumably *Parasphaerichthys*, and *Ctenops*. In all well-known species the body build and coloration differ only slightly between the sexes. Coloration is modest, even though the chocolate gourami's brownish white patterns often make them very distinctive.

All real mouthbrooders among the labyrinth fishes studied up to now produce the sinking type of egg. The eggs are heavier than water and opaque white. They are also relatively large and comparatively few in number. Female chocolate gouramis (*Sphaerichthys osphromenoides*) are mouthbrooders, so they make up a matriarchy. In the other species the male takes over hatching and care of the fry in his mouth. When the young leave their father's mouth, they are completely independent. Their father takes no further care of them and also does not normally chase after them.

3

# The Practical Labyrinth Fish Aquarium

First off, we must point out that there can not be any ideal labyrinth fish aquarium, but many different types (over 70) to match the number of known species. Every species has quite different needs in its own right, so the usual community tank is not suitable for many of them. In each case the reader should refer to the appropriate species description of his own fish to determine the proper conditions in which to keep them.

## A Community Tank for Labyrinth Fishes

You can keep a great number of labyrinth fishes in the usual community tank. The gourami specialist can even populate most of his tank with anabantoids. This chapter deals with such a community tank. The following chapter deals with aquarium supplies and equipment.

To me, a good community tank is an interestingly arranged, well-planted tank. Most labyrinth fishes, especially the often very colorful brooders, are made for just such an aquarium. Since they form territories, however, they are not completely without problems, and we have to account for this need.

*CAPACITY*: I'm going to talk about a 25-gallon tank, which comes standardized with sides about 32 inches long. This arrangement can apply just as well to tanks of up to 50 to 75 gallons with sides 40 to 48 inches long. With larger tanks you can be a little more generous when populating them, but be careful not to think that you can simply increase the number of species of fish proportionally to the increase in water volume.

*LOCATION*: A well-planted tropical aquarium is set up for 12 to 14 hours of light daily. A window gives too little light in winter and too much in summer, so we're going to rely on artificial lighting. The location will be a dark part of the room, thus taking into consideration the decorative effect of our artificially illuminated tank.

It's all the same to the fish whether we use incandescent bulbs, flourescent tubes, or high-pressure mercury lamps. It's merely a question of taste and money. The important thing is that the light burns about 13 hours a day and that the intensity is adequate for good plant growth. The rule of thumb is 0.5 watt of light per quart of water in the aquarium, but this can be exceeded.

In general, 40 watts is enough for a 25-gallon tank if the plants selected are not the kinds that need more light. The plants suggested here are almost all satisfactory in this respect.

*ACCESSORIES*: The tank needs an adjustable heater. Starting with an average room temperature of 68°F and aiming

for about 77°F, we need a 75-watt heater. Even if the system fails and the temperature climbs to over 80°F, our fish will survive. A 50-gallon tank needs a 100-watt heater, and a 75-gallon tank needs a 125-watt heater.

Labyrinth fishes are predominantly creatures of standing or only gently flowing water. A strong current is uncomfortable for them, so aeration has no place in our aquarium. In addition, aeration could deplete the tank of carbon dioxide, which would adversely affect plant growth. Good plant growth produces the necessary oxygen for the fish and bacterial decomposition, although we should note that this doesn't have too great an impact on our labyrinth fishes.

If you consider mild carbon dioxide fertilization necessary for your plant growth, then you can certainly do that in a tank of labyrinth fishes. I would, however, recommend using a filter. A filter is not necessary for the fish themselves, but provides for crystal-clear water by filtering out turbidity, thus fostering plant

The latest rage in aquariums is the mini-aquarium. This small tank is for the office desk, or as a night light in a child's room. The two tanks shown here are Hawkeye Aquariums which are sold in most pet shops. Your local pet shop will also have the necessary gravel, filters, and other paraphernalia which might be necessary for the proper establishment of the mini-tank. The tank above contains the gold variety of *Trichogaster trichopterus*, while the tank to the right contains a single male Siamese Fighting Fish.

This lovely Sea Clear is called an "Executive Aquarium." It contains concealed heating and filtering devices. It is available at most petshops.

growth. Even the (weak!) water current caused by filtering is good for fishes and plants alike because it prevents layers of different temperatures in the tank. It is, however, important that the current not be too strong, so we won't use any nozzles or anything similar. It's best to set the outlet (end of the water hose) right over the surface. The water should flow as a thick, "lazy" cascade into the tank.

Aside from a thermometer for regular temperature checks, we don't need any further technology beyond lighting, an adjustable heater, and a mild filter system. That's quite enough.

*BOTTOM*: Not so bright, relatively coarse sand has proven best as a bottom. The underlying layers don't have to be too thoroughly washed either. Clay ingredients here will help plant growth. The top inch or so, however, must be covered with thoroughly washed sand to avoid any turbidity.

A bottom like this can serve five or even ten years without going bad, but it only lasts that long if you keep Malayan live-bearing snails (*Melanoides tuberculata*) in the tank. These snails are completely harmless to fishes and plants and live down in the bottom, normally not even being noticed. They work the soil over constantly like good gardeners and keep anything from rotting down there.

Unfortunately, Malayan snails have the disagreeable characteristic of eventually leveling the bottom. That's not bad for the plants, but our tank decor looks better when the bottom climbs toward the background. We can compensate for the activity of the snails by stabilizing the ground with several large stones set right on the bottom plate before layering it with gravel. The gaps are filled with fine gravel. In this way we can form a stable bottom. The proportion of gravel to stone should be about equal in volume.

Avoid limestone and sand containing it. Limestone (chalk, calcium) gradually hardens the water, which is undesirable. To find out whether the sand or rocks contain calcium, a few drops of hydrochloric acid are dropped on a sample. If it foams it proves the material unsuitable for our tank.

*PLANTING AND DECORATION*: In "landscaping" our tank we want to keep the decor in mind, especially the plants and other accessories, so that everything is just right and well placed for our labyrinth fishes. Two large roots or pieces of driftwood are decisively decorative elements. More important, however, is their value as cover for our fish. A root in the back, in particular, makes it possible for persecuted or chased fish to hide directly at the water's surface. That's very important for labyrinth fishes, which regularly take in fresh air.

The roots can be bought as driftwood or similar material in pet shops. Soak them several days before putting them into the tank, so that they get waterlogged. You also can boil them to expel the gaseous contents of the old wood.

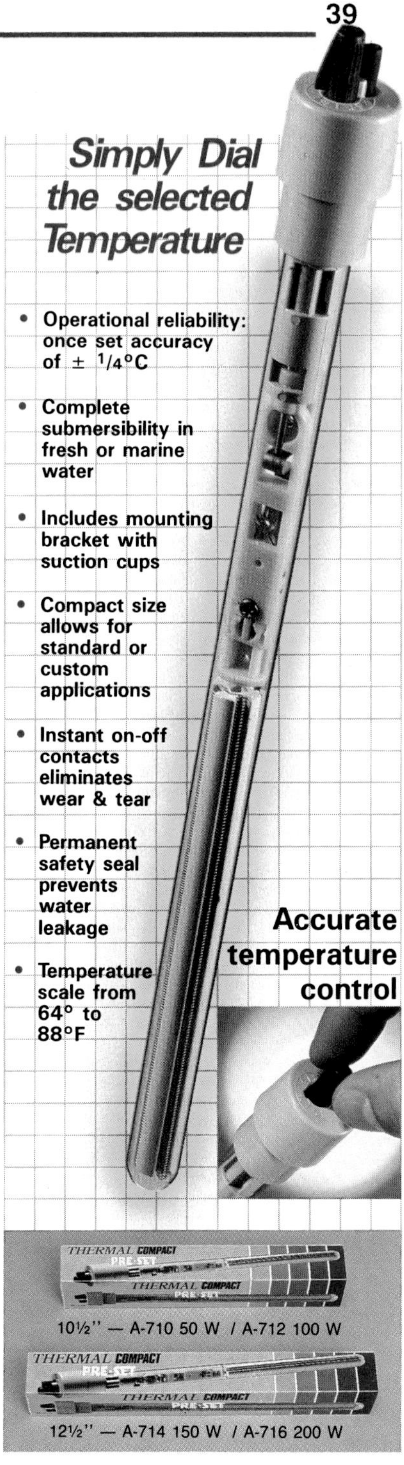
Simply Dial the selected Temperature
• Operational reliability: once set accuracy of ± 1/4°C
• Complete submersibility in fresh or marine water
• Includes mounting bracket with suction cups
• Compact size allows for standard or custom applications
• Instant on-off contacts eliminates wear & tear
• Permanent safety seal prevents water leakage
• Temperature scale from 64° to 88°F
Accurate temperature control
THERMAL COMPACT
PRE-SET
10½" — A-710 50 W / A-712 100 W
12½" — A-714 150 W / A-716 200 W

This advertisement appeared in most aquarium magazines and describes a wonderful heater. These heaters are available at your petshop. The author does not endorse this or any other product shown in this book.

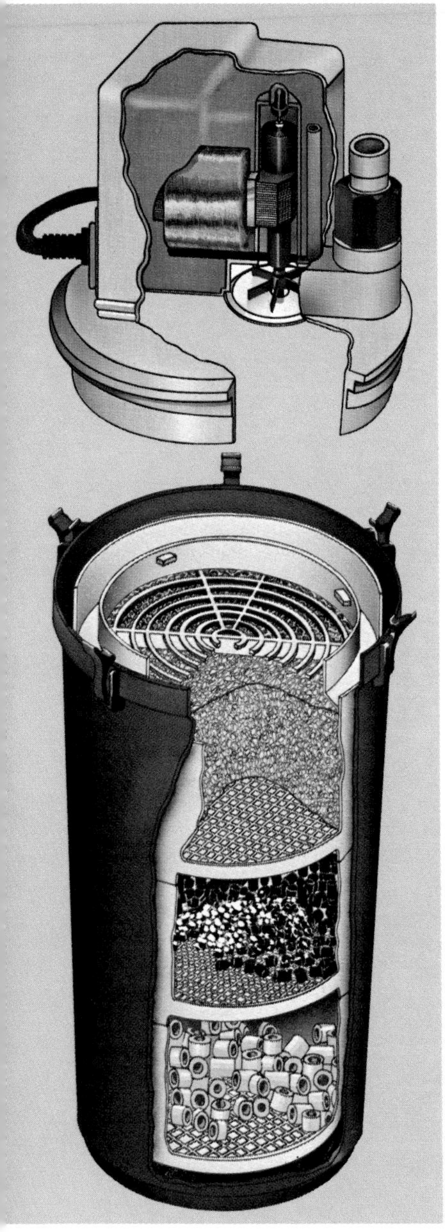

The most efficient filters are what are called "canister" filters. This exploded illustration shows a very popular canister filter which is available at most pet shops.

Always buy from your pet shop. Garden shops may sell chemically treated driftwood which poisons the aquarium.

Some anabantoids like to stay in "caves" or hollows at the bottom and build their bubblenests there under the cave roof. When installing the roots, take care to provide one or two caves or offer them at least a stone cover. Instead of that, we can give them half a coconut shell. The cave should have two openings, each at least as large as the total length of the proposed tenant. Caves like these are accepted as brooding spots by *Trichopsis* and *Pseudosphromenus* species as well as by *Betta smaragdina*. Pet shops sell special cave ornaments especially for this purpose.

The plants should divide up the available space so that the territorial fish can easily establish their territories. The better the space is subdivided into smaller areas, the more risk-free it will be to add several mutually competitive fish and species to the same tank.

Since the areas near the surface are more important for labyrinth fishes than the bottom zones, many plants are used that also grow up to the surface of the water, such as *Vallisneria*, *Hygrophila*, and tiger water lily. The plants mentioned here are very full and also relatively inexpensive. They are almost always available on the market. If, several weeks after planting, the aquarium vegetation grows to be extremely thick, our fish will only welcome it and feel right at home. Then, of course, you have to keep

trimming the *Vallisneria* and *Hygrophila*. Pet shops sell imitation plastic *Vallisneria* which serves the same purpose.

The tiger water lily, too, will send floating leaves upward. We can leave that one alone. It'll give the labyrinth fish an opportunity to build their nests under the floating leaves of this water lily. The plant, however, does cut off a lot of light from the plants at lower levels, but that's not so bad because I suggest *Cryptocoryne* species and Java fern, which get along on very low levels of light, for down there.

For floating plants, I recommend a medium-sized Sumatra fern, *Ceratopteris thalictroides,* just the ideal plant for labyrinth fishes, many of which like to build their bubblenests under the leaves. Sumatra fern is a full-growing plant and propagates well. It needs, like *Vallisneria* and *Hygrophila*, the timely hand of the gardner. The *Cryptocoryne* and Java fern, however, need a lot of tranquility, and once planted should not be disturbed much.

This basic landscaping can, of course, be modified. *Vallisneria* can be replaced by a thicket of *Limnophila indica*, *Hygrophila* by water wisteria (*Hygrophila difformis*) or *Ludwigia*.

I prefer plants from the Asian tropics, but you can also use American plants. Instead of the tiger water lily, for example, there are the Amazonian swordplants (*Echinodorus bleheri*, *E. parviflorus*, or *E. horizontalis*), and instead of *Vallisneria* there's a group of *Cabomba*. The fish themselves, in any case, do not place any value on geographically

(Above): When starting a new aquarium, it is often helpful to use a starting solution which removes harmful chemicals and stimulates helpful organisms. (Below): The Diatom filter is the most efficient in that it picks up very small particles from the water. Pet shops usually have many types of filters to show you.

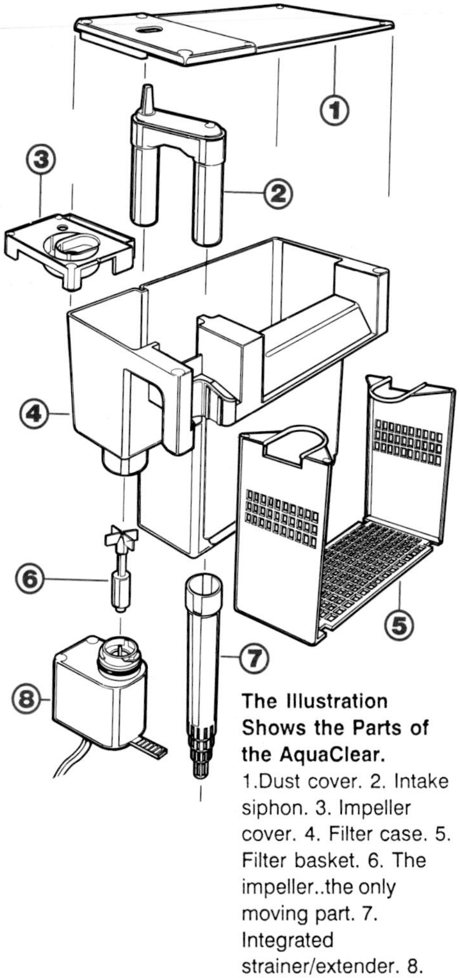


**The Illustration Shows the Parts of the AquaClear.**
1.Dust cover. 2. Intake siphon. 3. Impeller cover. 4. Filter case. 5. Filter basket. 6. The impeller..the only moving part. 7. Integrated strainer/extender. 8. Hermetically sealed motor.

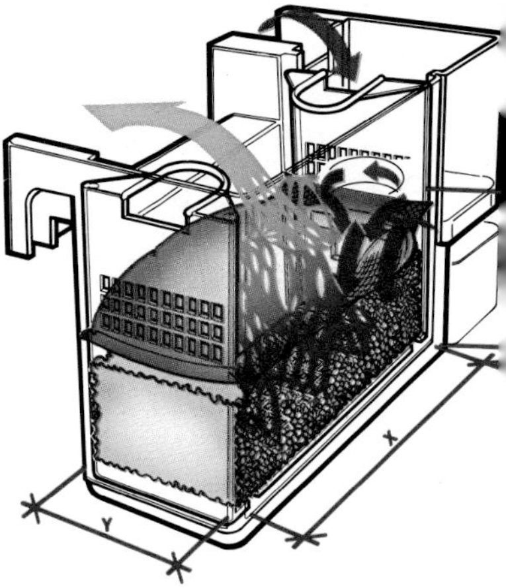


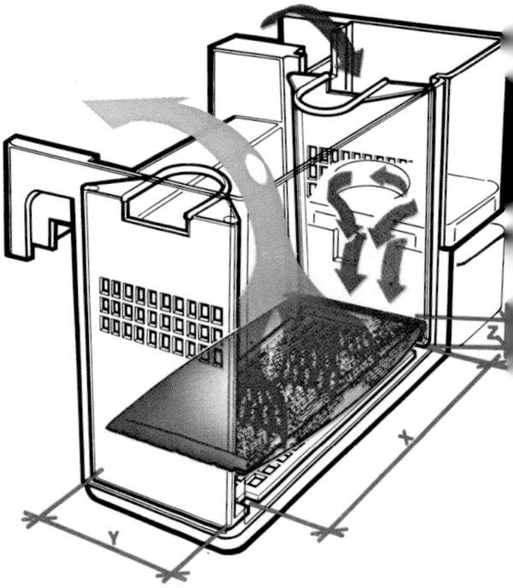

This AquaClear Cycle Guard (trade names) comes in various sizes. You can calculate the filter medium area by multiplying the dimensions X x Y x Z to get the volume of filtering medium. This is a test which should be performed if filtering is necessary in your aquarium.

proper vegetation.

*WATER VALUES*: The water values for our general purpose labyrinth tank are: temperature: 77° to 79°F; pH: slightly acidic (6 to 7.2); hardness: up to 20, but preferably 15 or lower.

## Community and Socialization Recommendations

Most labyrinth fishes become territorial just at the moment when they feel particularly comfortable. The pet shop usually keeps them together in large tanks, and there are no problems there. We can also pack 20 dwarf gouramis and another 20 mosaic gouramis into a bare tank, but this scene will hardly satisfy us. I'll illustrate with an actually verified example of just what the relationship is between territoriality and number of individuals in a certain defined space.

I had a small aquarium whose bottom measured 11 × 6 inches and had a water level of 4 to 6 inches. It held two *Colisa labiosa* males meant for breeding. The tank was divided by flat, vertically placed rocks and aquatic plants. After the fish were introduced into the tank, fights broke out all over for a day until the strongest had taken possession of the back, more secure, and darker half of the aquarium which was best protected. The just slightly less dominant fish established an approximately equal-sized territory in the other half of the aquarium.

The fish soon built bubblenests that became the centers of their territories. It's interesting to note that the two territories were as far apart as possible.

Only the extreme arrangement of space in the tank made it possible in this case for the two gouramis to build their nests. If a

Labyrinth fishes require a reasonably clean, secure environment if you expect them to thrive. A balanced community tank is best, but a special labyrinth tank is also good. This theoretical tank shown below is a fine example of a labyrinth aquarium. Drawn by Burkhard Kahl after the author.

third male had been introduced, the two fish with territories already established would have persecuted the newcomer something awful. The relatively least dangerous spot is the furthest one from both of the already established territorial centers—right on the border between the territories, down on the bottom—and that is where a third introduced fish actually found refuge (which, by the way, was pre-planned with protective rocks just for this purpose). After a few days the third male was able to set up a mini-territory on the bottom and finally even gain a small piece of surface territory, which was, of course, exactly between the two territories of the original tenants.

The surface part of the territory is important for labyrinth fishes. There was not enough room there, though, to build a bubblenest in the small tank. If I had added still another male gourami, then there really wouldn't have been enough room, and their "atmosphere" would have been charged with unrest. All territory owners would have had to give up their territories. Fights would have ceased, and the fish would have formed a school.

This example demonstrates that a tank must be well organized, and that you should keep the number of fish low if you want to observe typical labyrinth fish behavior. A community tank must be designed so that several labyrinth fish can be kept together with relatively few problems. In fish rivalry, the closer their relationship, the sooner they encroach upon one another.

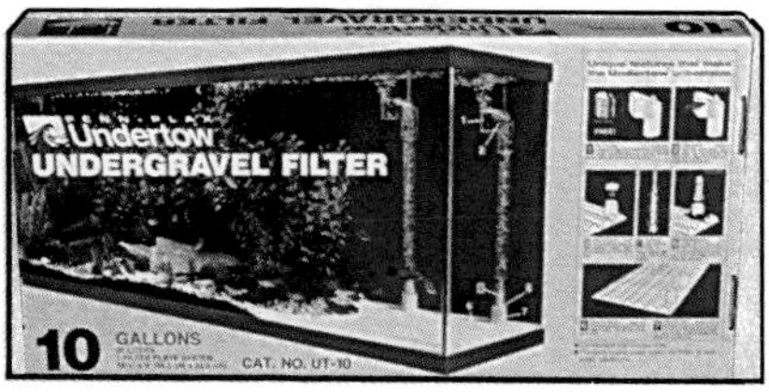


Undergravel filtration systems are based upon water being gently sucked through the gravel substrate. They have many advantages over other mechanical filters...as well as some disadvantages. Discuss your particular needs with your pet shop operator to get the filtration system best suited for your own situation.

I've developed a plan that is certainly helpful in making up the labyrinth community. I've classified these into three groups depending upon their needs and behavior. **Group I** includes the fishes that stay near the surface and produce floating eggs. **Group II** contains the fishes that prefer the bottom and produce sinking eggs. **Group III** contains *Betta splendens* and *B. smaragdina.*

**Group I**

-Dwarf gourami (*Colisa lalia*) 2/3*

-Honey gourami (*Colisa sota*) 2/3

-Thick-lipped gourami (*Colisa labiosa*) 2/3

-Striped, banded or giant gourami (*Colisa fasciata*) 1/2

-Moonlight gourami (*Trichogaster microlepis*) 1/2

-Three-spot gourami (*Trichogaster trichopterus*) 1/2

-Paradisefish (*Macropodus opercularis*) 1/2

-Black paradisefish (*Macropodus concolor*) 1/2

In the top sketch, two male Dwarf Gouramis divide an aquarium into two areas with an invisible fence marking each territory (A and B). The center of each territory is the bubblenest built to attract a female and prepare for spawning. When a third male Dwarf Gourami is introduced, he will claim a separate territory marked (C). It straddles the invisible fence separating territories (A) and (B). Drawn by M. Bertsch from sketches by the author. Redrawn by John R. Quinn.

**Group II**

-Croaking gourami (*Trichopsis vittatus*) 2/2

-Red sharp-tailed paradisefish (*Pseudosphromenus dayi*) 2/2

-Javanese mouthbrooding fighting fish (*Betta picta*) 2/2

-Penang mouthbrooding fighting fish (*Betta pugnax*) 1/1

**Group III**

-Siamese fighting fish (*Betta splendens*) 1/2

-Emerald fighting fish (*Betta smaragdina*) 1/2

**The numbers following the species name indicate how many males (before the slash) we should really introduce into the tank, followed by the number of females. If the fish are available only in couples, or if the sex is unknown, then it's better to take one fish too few than too many.*

Now we can select the appropriate combinations for each species from each group. We've got to be cautious, however, within the groups. If we consider the proportions, then we also can combine here, such as only one *T. vittatus* pair plus a pair of red sharp-tailed paradisefish instead of two *Trichopsis vittatus* pairs. We've got to understand that these combinations do not guarantee peace. It could happen that all males simultaneously feel like breeding, so the available space will not be adequate at all. At the beginning, especially, we should be alert and ready to "fish out" any persecuted fish and remove it to safety.

For variety, I would include a few non-labyrinth fishes in our labyrinth tank. I would recommend two or three flying foxes (*Epalzeorhynchus*) and a small school of perhaps eight harlequin rasboras *(Rasbora heteromorpha)* as helpful little cleaners. For 50- or 75-gallon tanks, I'd recommend first the combinations and individual numbers discussed above, and then, only after several weeks, determine whether additional fish might fit into the

An ideal small aquarium setup for labyrinth fish. There are plenty of hiding places and floating leaves under which bubblenests can be constructed, and the tank is attractive enough for general purposes. Drawn by John R. Quinn.

community. In principle, a labyrinth fish tank can be too small, but never too large! The larger the tank, the greater the possibilities for community life. In the often gigantic exhibition tanks of public aquariums you can see really daring combinations that usually are not feasible in smaller home aquarium tanks.

## Special Aquaria for Labyrinth Fishes

The community aquarium is not suitable for many labyrinth fishes. Typical herbivores such as *Osphronemus* or *Anabas* would go into a tank set up predominantly with rocks and roots, but you should at least try to include *Riccia*, Java moss (*Vesicularia dubyana*), and water sprite. These plants usually remain undisturbed. Other labyrinth fishes, on the other hand, always spare plants, but they grow so large that in 25-gallon tanks they don't tolerate other fishes, at least not during spawning. I'm thinking here of *Belontia* species. For them, the typical community tank set up (without other fishes) would be an ideal breeding tank.

For a community built around *Belontia* species, you can introduce a large climbing perch such as *Ctenopoma kingsleyae*, but also good are medium-sized cichlids from South and Central America. You can set up a 100-gallon or 125-gallon tank quite well for cichlids by using rocks, roots, and hardy plants. If you add a fully grown *Belontia* pair, they can really protect the plants; they keep their territory clear of all other fishes, even of plant-eating cichlids.

If you want to keep sensitive small labyrinth fishes, it's best to

Most pet shops carry everything necessary to start a labyrinth fish aquarium. Some manufacturers pre-package a balanced starter kit for a 10-gallon aquarium (an ideal size for many anabantoids). It is usually much cheaper to buy a starter kit.

Kissing Gouramis, *Helostoma temmincki*, spawning. Photo by H.-J. Richter.

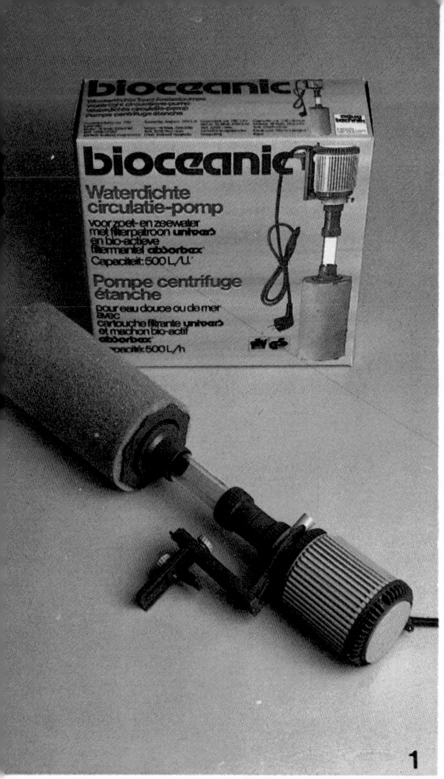
bioceanic
Waterdichte circulatie-pomp
voor zoet- en zeewater met filterpatroon unicarb en bio-actieve filtermantel absorbex
Capaciteit: 500 L/U.
Pompe centrifuge étanche
pour eau douce ou de mer avec cartouche filtrante unicarb et machon bio-actif absorbex
Capacité: 500 L/h
1

AMMO-CARB
UNDER GRAVEL
FILTER CARTRIDGE
(Giant Refillable Cartridge)
AQUARIUM PHARMACEUTICALS INC
2

Kreiselpumpenfilter
ZWEIKAMMER-FILTERSYSTEM
von
NUOVA
aquatechnik
ZWEIKAMMER-FILTERSYSTEM
450
NUOVA
aquatechnik
3

The AUTOMATIC AQUARIUM WATER CHANGER
BETTER THAN ANY FILTERING METHOD!
AUTOMATIC WATER CHANGER
GREATEST INNOVATION SINCE THE GLASS AQUARIUM
Ready to use--installs in seconds
• No electricity
• No moving parts
• Works on any size tank
The AUTOMATIC AQUARIUM WATER CHANGER
4

do so in smaller tanks that under some circumstances can be as small as 7½ gallons. These mini-tanks are more difficult to manage because small changes have greater effects in smaller tanks, so I wouldn't recommend them for beginners. They do, however, have the advantages that valuable small fish can be controlled better and you can feed them individually with live foods without tankmates grabbing too much of it. Whoever has problems with obtaining soft water will come to appreciate these mini-tanks, in which, by the way, partial water changes have to be made more frequently than is usual with others.

A mini-tank can be arranged attractively. A small plastic root or stump looks nice, and small living plant species can be used. I'd recommend *Cryptocoryne affinis*.

An aquarium like this can be inhabited by two different labyrinth species that stay (relatively) out of each other's way. A proven combination with excellent results is honey gouramis (two females, one male) and three or four red sharp-tailed paradisefish or croaking dwarf gouramis. The honey gouramis keep mainly to the upper layers, and both of the other species are more comfortable lower in the tank.

Pet shops carry accessories to make aquarium-keeping easier. As examples of such items we have (1) a waterproof circulation pump; (2) a special filter cartridge for an undergravel filter which is refillable; (3) a double-chambered power filter; (4) an automatic water changer which is an absolute essential!

## Feeding

In the wild, the labyrinth fish diet is quite varied. In the aquarium, most can be easily trained to eat dry food; newly captured fish do cause some difficulty, but those are exceptions and are rarely offered for sale. Such fish must be fed live foods, which you can collect or buy at your local pet shop.

If possible, give all your labyrinth fishes live foods at least occasionally. It's even necessary for breeding many species. Have no fear of introducing any pathogens into the aquarium—it's far more probable that fish fed on a varied diet will be more resistant to infections than are fish fed on a one-sided diet. Never feed just one brand of dry food. Use different manufacturers.

Earthworms are excellent live food for large labyrinth fishes, especially edible gouramis, *Anabas*, *Belontia*, *Sandelia*, and climbing perches. Climbing perches eat earthworms about their own length. Large *Betta* species also relish eating earthworms.

Feeding kissing gouramis is a problem. These fish are primarily plankton filter-feeders, and thus are adapted to a biotope other than the crystal-clear water of an aquarium. It's best to feed them finely crushed dry food with high plant content several times a day. Freshly hatched *Artemia* (brine shrimp), too, are liked.

## Breeding

If we keep our labyrinth fishes properly, we can see many species spawn in the community

tank. The young, however, won't grow up under those conditions. Tankmates often make a meal of the eggs even during spawning. In many cases, though, we can fish out a bubblenest with eggs or larvae from a not too thickly populated community tank and transfer it to a separate tank with water of the same temperature and composition. That's the first

(Above):There are many excellent fish foods. The most popular types are flakes. Feed your fish as many DIFFERENT manufacturers' brands of fish food as possible. (Below): The ideal labyrinth fish aquarium must have an almost airtight cover system. Between the reflector and the aquarium, a glass cover will insure that the bubblenest is not disturbed by air pollution and dirt.

step to rearing the little labyrinth fish.

As a rule, however, labyrinth fishes are set up for breeding in a separate tank. It's clear that what we want is a set of optimal circumstances. If we separate the fish that are meant for breeding and feed them well, then the actual breeding usually occurs with very little difficulty. The prerequisite, however, is that the fish are ready to spawn.

upside-down flowerpot (with an entry hole in it) provides refuge for the female. Some species, usually the sinking-egg producers, also use the flowerpot as a brood cave. Pet shops sell artificial plastic caves.

Nest-builders usually spawn during the afternoon. Following that, the female should be taken out. Leave the father with the brood until the fry swim free, then remove him, too. At this point

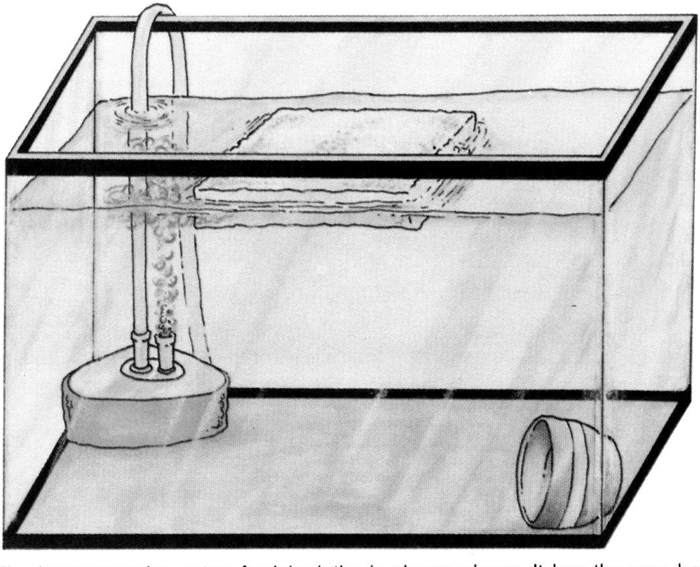

The least attractive setup for labyrinths is shown above. It has the very bare essentials, yet it serves ideally for raising the young. The small flowerpot laying on its side provides a safe refuge for a battered bride. The sponge filter will prevent fry from being sucked out of the tank. The floating piece of styrofoam is the base for a bubblenest. Drawn by John Quinn.

A breeding tank for nest-builders is, at best, a fully set-up, well-planted aquarium. It's very important to provide sufficient hiding spots where the initially very persecuted female can take refuge. Note again that a breeding tank can never be too large! The fish are, of course, introduced in pairs. In addition, a pint-sized,

begin fine aeration (that is, tiny pearl-like bubbles).

Non-nest-builders are set up for breeding in the largest tanks possible. These are planted with good floating vegetation *(Riccia)* but also have a lot of plant-free swimming room. They spawn in late evening or at night, so the surface should be searched for

eggs every morning. The older fish are egg eaters and have to be removed after spawning.

Rearing of the young succeeds best in older established tanks, because a rich microfauna is already present. Otherwise, feeding the young could present problems during the first six days. It's best to provide rotifers or other protozoans you buy, catch or culture yourself. Most young in a few days after becoming free-swimming eat freshly hatched *Artemia* nauplii. These brine shimp larvae can be easily hatched from eggs that are available at your pet shop. Instructions for hatching the brine shrimp eggs are on the packages.

Soon, the young can be fed with finely minced *Tubifex* worms or other fine foods. Take care, however, that gouramis do not receive any food containing glassworm larvae. The gouramis

A meager, but improved commercial spawning tank for labyrinth fishes is shown above. It is the same as the bare tank shown on the previous page but substrate and plants have been added. Drawn by John R. Quinn.

eat these "glass rods" but misjudge their size and choke on them. The half-swallowed larvae hang out of their mouths and obstruct the passage of air into the labyrinth organ. This danger does not exist for the young of sinking-egg producers. Ask your pet shop for advice on live foods.

The uninterrupted growth of the young does not depend upon only sufficient and varied feeding. If the breeding tank was small, we've got to think of a timely transfer to larger tanks. In addition, a partial water change should be made if possible every two days by exchanging about a third of the water for fresher water of the same temperature and quality.

## Disease

With a varied diet (including, when possible, live foods), regular partial water changes (a third monthly), and good accommodations, our labyrinth fishes will be among the hardiest ornamental fishes. The chocolate gourami is really the only problem fish in the trade because it is prone to illness.

The two most frequent pathogens are *Ichthyophthirius* and *Oodinium*, both microscopic protozoans mostly found on the skin. In the case of *Ichthyophthirius*, we can recognize the parasites as white dots on the skin or fins of the fish. *Oodinium* can also be recognized by the tiny white dots, but much smaller ones—the affected fish seems to be covered with fine confectioner's sugar, at least in the final stages. The first stages are difficult to detect. The earliest hint of *Oodinium* is the fish's behavior; affected fish retreat apathetically with fins pressed together.

Fish can be treated easily for both diseases with commercially available medications. Non-treated fish usually die. Moreover, they infect their tankmates. Follow the instructions for use closely! *Oodinium*, especially, is a parasite

*Colisa chuna* infected with either *Ichthyophthirius* or *Oodinium* infection. These infections are both characterized by white spots peppered over the body of the fish including its eyes! It is almost impossible to identify the parasite without a microscope. Photo by Dr. Herbert R. Axelrod.

of weakness and debility that mainly attacks fishes that are on a one-sided diet and are kept too cold. This pathogenic organism is most common in soft water.

Many times you can notice knot-like growths, often white, on the fins of imported fishes. They "eat up" the fins and lead eventually to the death of the fish. The causative agent of this *Lymphocystis* disease is an intracellular virus. Since *Lymphocystis* is very contagious, the affected fish should be isolated. There are medications on the market, but the treatment is long and drawn out. This disease is observed mostly in imported gouramis.

Another disease frequently occurring in gouramis is rarely noticed by aquarists. The pathogens are microscopic skin and gill worms of the genus *Dactylogyrus*. They can be seen under the microscope to be small, transparent trematode worms. A powerful hooking mechanism on the rear of the parasite, as well as four black eyespots on the anterior portion, are characteristic. When half-grown *Trichogaster* only grow a little despite good feeding, one should always suspect *Dactylogyrus*. These runts often die off without any outward signs of disease. Even the fry are not safe from *Dactylogyrus*. I've seen these parasites in *Trichogaster microlepis* where after two days

(Above): Petshops carry a large selection of excellent air pumps. Disconnect all filters when treating an aquarium and just use an airpump with an air releaser to aerate the water. (Left): Brine shrimp eggs, when hatched, make an excellent food for gouramis and almost all other fry. Don't feed brine shrimp nauplii (*Artemia*) while medicating the aquarium. The medicine might kill the nauplii and the fish might ingest these poisoned creatures.

free-swimming worm larvae were released from the gill regions of the fry. Well-kept fish are normally able to hold down the number of their *Dactylogyrus* parasites by as yet unknown means. Only after damage by cold or other parasites, as a rule, is there a massive increase in gill worms, with a fatal outcome.

Carefully isolate any fish with swollen bellies, wounds, abscesses, or popeyes. We have to assume that the fish are infected with *Ichthyosporidium*, a treacherous fungus, or with fish tuberculosis. These diseases are

Petshops carry a huge variety of aquarium medications. Different areas of the world have different laws governing the use of antibiotics for aquarium fishes and who is able to dispense them. You must check with your local petshop about which drugs may legally treat your fish problem. One of the main reasons for dealing with a petshop rather than buying aquarium products from a self-service rack or display in a large supermarket or variety chain store is that there is someone who can answer your questions.

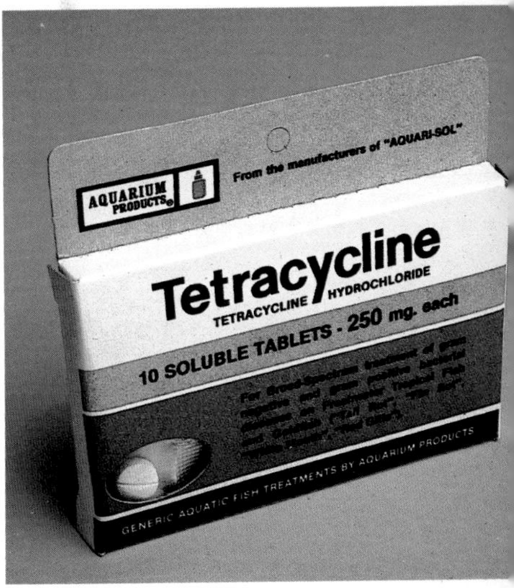

difficult to diagnose and there is only slight hope of a cure.

Sunken or emaciated bellies are often a sign of senility in fish. Many labyrinth fishes, such as the dwarf gourami *Colisa lalia*, live to be only two years old. Others can live to be ten or more years old, like *Osphronemus*, *Belontia*, or large climbing perches. As a rule of thumb, you can consider that the natural life expectancy of labyrinth fish species increases as their body size increases.

There are many different filters available at pet shops. The sponge filter has the advantage that it cannot suck fry into the filtering unit. However, these filters can only be effective in small aquariums unless more than one is used at a time. They must be cleaned regularly to be effective. On the other hand, a large motor driven filter can probably clean 50 times more water than a sponge filter, but it creates currents by bringing water into the filter and driving it out at high speeds. This is dangerous for fry and should not be used on a breeding aquarium. Motor-driven pumps and filters are ideal for community aquariums and larger setups.

# Genera and Species

Seventeen genera and about 70 currently known species of labyrinth fish are discussed in this section. Groups of symbols and numbers accompanying the species descriptions contain identification, maintenance, and breeding information. The upper line contains aquarium data, and the lower line contains taxonomic information. Reading from left to right, the figures in the first line are for total length, temperature requirements, aquarium setup, maintenance **(H),** breeding **(Z),** and availability **(A).**

**total length**. Maximum body length of the species from lips to the end of the caudal fin. The male is to the left of the slash, the female to the right of the slash. The small species usually reach the given length only in the aquarium. Large species reach the given length only in large tanks. Lengths are rendered in centimeters here.

**temperature**. Optimal maintenance temperature is to the left of the slash, optimal breeding temperature to the right of the slash. These values fluctuate even in the fish's native habitat, so they can only be a guideline. Maintenance temperatures can also vary by 3-4°F (2°C) above or below the given temperature for long periods. The Centigrade scale is used in this group of symbols. In the text discussions, the temperatures are given in Fahrenheit.

**aquarium setup. I** for community life in large, well-planted tanks; size of tank and inhabitants must be compatible. **II** put into well-planted tanks if possible; mini-tanks can be used for the smaller species. **III** with as many others of the same species as possible; community with other species of fish of appropriate size is possible.

**(H) degree of difficulty in holding. H1** easy. **H2** moderately easy. **H3** difficult, requiring proper accommodations. Difficulties can occur because of greater demands upon the water conditions or the diet.

**(Z) difficulty in breeding. Z1** easy. **Z2** moderately easy. **Z3** difficult.

**(A) availability. A1** regularly in the trade. **A2** sporadically in the trade. **A3** only exceptionally found in the trade and normally available only from specialists. **A4** not yet imported alive.

It's obvious that the information on maintenance and breeding can only be given for species that have already been kept in an aquarium. It's also obvious that the availability is subject to transient changes. Regional circumstances may be involved. The description of the species is purposely kept short, particularly when pictures can say more. Great importance was placed upon sexual differentiation, knowledge of which is essential for keeping as well as, of course,

for breeding these fishes. In general, however, these differences only become apparent in sexually mature fish.

The data in the second group indicate dorsal fin rays **(D),** anal fin rays **(A)** and number of scales along the middle longitudinal row **(mLR).** The banded climbing perch, for example, is:

**D:**XVI/8-9; **A:**X/9-11; **mLR:**27-28,

whereby:

**(D)** *dorsal fin rays.* The dorsal fin normally has 16 hard spines (shown in Roman numerals) followed by 8-9 soft rays.

**(A)** *anal fin rays.* The anal fin likewise has hard spines and soft rays reported as for the dorsals, in this case 10 spines and 9–11 rays.

**(mLR)** *number of scales* in a middle longitudinal series beginning at the rear margin of the gill cover and continuing to the base of the caudal fin.

The scientific names of the fish are also important for aquarists, specially when rare species are concerned. Every name consists of a capitalized generic name and a second non-capitalized species name. The names are all Latinized, regardless of the language from which they originated.

In discussion of the genera and the species, I have given the source or translation of the name. The translation, however, is often of only theoretical interest, for in many cases the meaning is anything but pertinent, such as, for example, *Betta imbellis* with a translation of peaceful fighting fish! The scientific names, however, are binding according to the rules of nomenclature regardless of whether the actual words make sense or not.

## AFRICAN LABYRINTH FISHES

The African labyrinth fishes come from the slowly flowing jungle waters of the Congo basin as well as from the sun-drenched savannah creeks of the northern zones and from the almost oxygenless bog puddles and swampy areas of East Africa. In South Africa, some labyrinth fishes even live in very rapidly flowing, cool trout streams.

The approximately 30 African species are grouped into only two genera. The main portion consists of the climbing perches (*Ctenopoma*), which are limited to the tropical zones. Geographically separated from them are the South African *Sandelia*, occupying the extreme tip of the continent. A third genus—*Oshimia* or *Micracanthus*—of which only a single specimen was described was discovered to be an error. Investigation by Roberts in 1981 showed that a *Betta splendens* female must have been mistakingly included in an African collection and described as a new genus and species.

African labyrinth fishes are unfortunately only rarely available commercially.

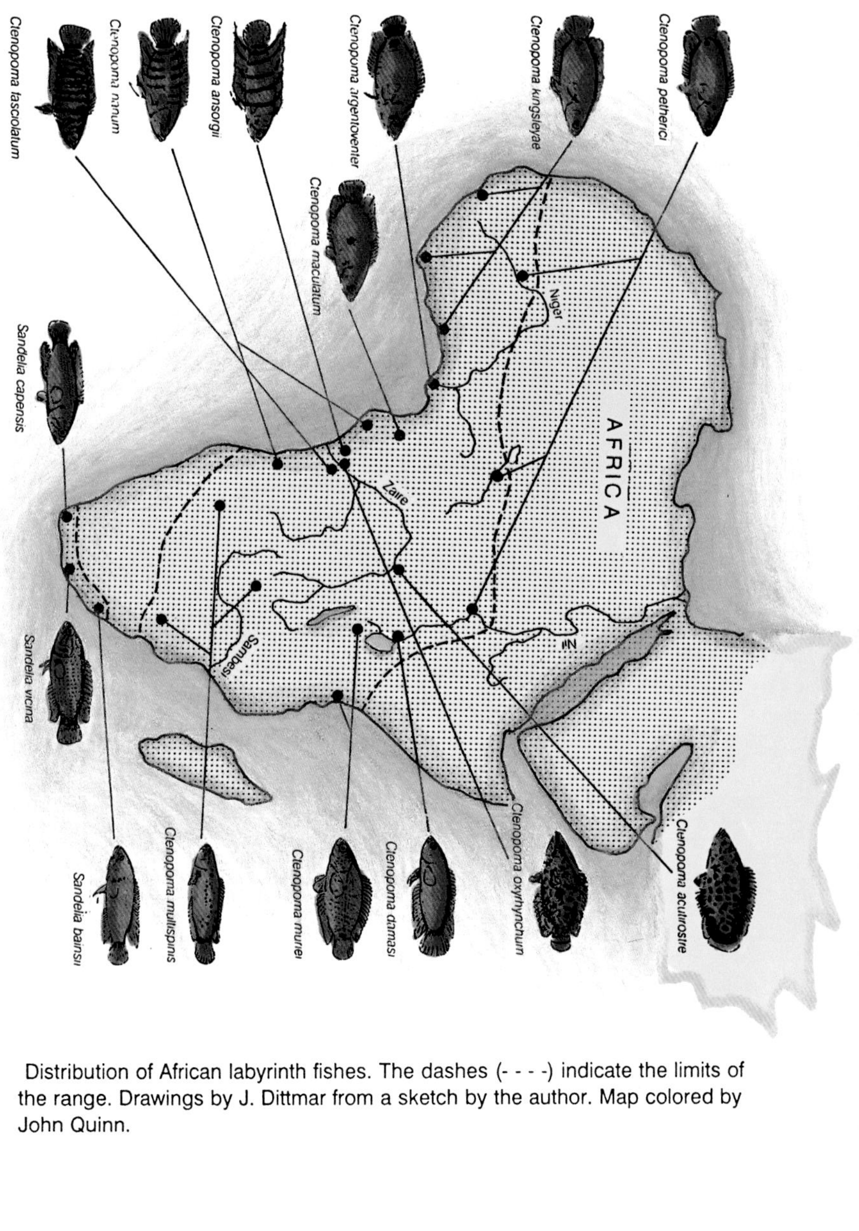


Distribution of African labyrinth fishes. The dashes (- - - -) indicate the limits of the range. Drawings by J. Dittmar from a sketch by the author. Map colored by John Quinn.

# Genus *Ctenopoma*

**Peters, 1844**

**CLIMBING PERCHES**

**Number of species**: With approximately 30 species, this is the largest anabantoid genus.

**Systematics**: *Ctenopoma*: Ktenos (Greek) = comb; poma (Greek) = cover; "Comb-cover" because of the comb-like serrations of the gill cover.

**Family**: Anabantidae.

**Distribution**: Rainforests and savannahs of tropical Africa.

**Characteristics**: Climbing perches have serrated margins on their gill covers. When danger threatens, they spread the gill covers, which catch easily in the nets set out to catch them, often making it difficult to free them uninjured from the mesh. It's better to catch them with a large bottle under water. All climbing perches like to retreat into the shadows, and this behavior should be taken into consideration when planning an aquarium. They feel particularly comfortable over a soft bottom, ideally peat.

Two or three groups can be distinguished by their ecology and behavior (Peters, 1976). One group includes relatively small bubblenest-builders with often striking coloration in the territorial males. They are shy fishes that like to stay in thick vegetation.

To the other group belong the non-brooders, which often grow larger. They are less shy fishes of open water that like to swim, especially in schools. When mating, they embrace only briefly. The fully grown males have spinous areas that apparently facilitate rapid attachment to the female when mating. The spinous areas consist of a group of scales with very serrated margins, recognizable on a living fish only when it is taken out of the water. Older females also can have these spinous areas, but they are much less pronounced than in the males.

Studies by Berns & Peters (1968) show that there are two

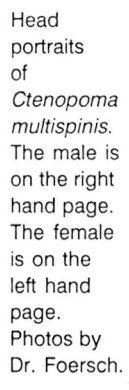

Head portraits of *Ctenopoma multispinis.* The male is on the right hand page. The female is on the left hand page. Photos by Dr. Foersch.

types of non-brooders. Males of the somewhat more compact species such as *Ctenopoma muriei* and *Ctenopoma petherici* have two spinous areas, one right behind the eye and one at the base of the tail. The very slim species such as *Ctenopoma multispinis* and *Ctenopoma pellegrini*, on the other hand, only have the anterior spinous areas. The slim types may mate in a somewhat different manner than the other non-brooders. More precise details are not known in this case.

These behavioral groupings apparently lend insight into the phylogeny of these fishes. Thorough anatomical investigation by Elsen (1976) supports this view. Independently of Peters and Berns, and about simultaneously with them, Elsen classified the climbing perches into three groups, based mainly upon the anatomy of the labyrinth organ and the labyrinth cavity, that nicely confirm the correctness of the behavioral classification:

**multispinis-Group**

(*Ctenopoma multispinis*, *C. pellegrini*, *C. nigropannosum*): Large labyrinth cavity and well developed labyrinth organ. Transitional to the genus *Anabas*, which is similar in build and behavior (especially *C. multispinis's* cross-country movement). This group corresponds to the group of slim non-brooders that lack the posterior spinous areas.

**petherici-Group**

(*Ctenopoma petherici*, *C. kingsleyae*, *C. ocellatum*, *C. acutirostre*, *C. maculatum*, *C. oxyrhynchum*: Transitional to the genus *Sandelia*. Includes non-brooding climbing perches with anterior and posterior spinous areas.

**congicum-Group**

(*Ctenopoma congicum*, *C. fasciolatum*, *C. nanum*, *C. ctenotis*, *C. damasi*, *C. davidae*, *C. muriei*): Body build midway between the other two groups.

Includes bubblenest-building climbing perches. *Ctenopoma muriei* and possibly *C. davidae* don't fit well into this group but should really be assigned to the *petherici-group*.

Neither Elsen nor Peters & Berns found in their admittedly incomplete though very detailed scientific findings, any reason to split the genus *Ctenopoma*, which is certainly a noteworthy fact for those who—with much weaker evidence—wanted to split the genus *Betta*.

All imported climbing perches, and briefly also many other species, are in this book. The remaining species will be mentioned only here:

*Ctenopoma ashbysmithi* Banister and Bailey, 1979 from Kindu, Zaire;

*C. breviventralis* (Pellegrin, 1938) from an unknown locality;

*C. davidae* (Poll, 1939) from the Congo near Brazzaville (Stanley Pool);

*C. garuanum* (Ahl, 1927) from the Cameroons;

*C. intermedium* (Pellegrin, 1920) from the Zambezi;

*C. pekkolai* (Rendal, 1935) from the White Nile;

*C. riggenbachi* (Ahl, 1927) from the Cameroons;

*C. togoensis* (Ahl, 1928) from Togo.

Species status is not 100% certain for all the species mentioned above.

## *Ctenopoma acutirostre* Pellegrin, 1899

**Systematics**: First described in *Bull. Mus. Paris*, p. 360.

**acutirostre**: with pointed snout.

**Description**: Sexual differences: Spinous areas of male. Most deep-bodied of all climbing perches. Very compressed laterally. Soft portions of caudal, anal, and dorsal fins with narrow transparent margins covered with small scales. Sharp-nosed fish with large, striking eyes. Ground color light beige with dark brown, irregularly distributed spots. Spotted climbing perches can also be transiently uniformly dark brown, especially older fish.

**Distribution**: Upper and middle reaches of the Congo along the bank zones of the tributaries and deep pools. According to Gartner (1983) also in Cameroon. First introduced into Germany in 1955.

**Maintenance**: Very quiet fish that often stay motionless under cover. Completely peaceful toward others of the same species and any other small fishes (as long as they do not qualify as food). This species is not very difficult to keep under proper conditions, preferably a large species tank that shouldn't be too bright. Provide a thick, light-absorbing floating plant cover of *Ceratopteris* (water sprite) along with many hiding spots among the roots, which should reach up to the surface of the water.

The fish are fearful and don't feed well in the presence of equally large but more active fishes. They have done well in communities with the somewhat smaller but not as shy *Ctenopoma oxyrhynchum*.

Fully grown spotted climbing perch like to eat smaller fishes,

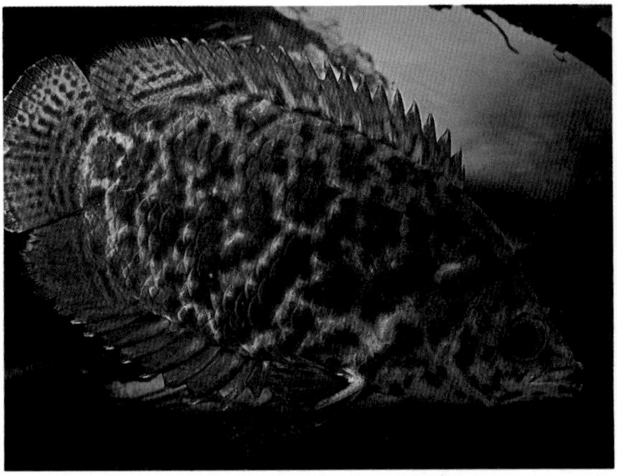

*Ctenopoma acutirostre.* Photo by B. Kahl.

*Ctenopoma acutirostre* PELLEGRIN, 1899

| | | | | | |
|---|---|---|---|---|---|
| 15 cm | 25/27° C | II/III | H2 | Z3 | A 2 |
| D XIV–XVIII/9–12 | | A IX–X/10 | | | mLR 26–28 |

which they only chase, however, if they are very hungry. Prey is normally seized with a surprise thrust. They can be trained to take small and medium-sized earthworms, water beetles, mealworms, and other live food. You can also substitute a little tuna or minced cooked lean ham. Young fish satisfy themselves first with water fleas and mosquito larvae.

**Breeding**: No breeding success has yet been achieved by hobby aquarists. Free spawners. A chance breeding was successful in 1982 at the Basle Zoo (Nann, 1983). The thickly planted tank offered many hiding spots and was also populated by *Polypterus* sp. (bichirs) and a school of *Micralestes interruptus* (Congo tetras). Tank capacity was about 1980 gallons (approximately 8×7×5 feet) at 78.8°F and 3° hardness. Despite the predatory fish, 10 to 15 young *Ctenopoma* reached 0.6 to 1.2 inches length (end of November, 1982). The parents were over ten years old.

## *Ctenopoma ansorgii* (Boulenger, 1912)

**Systematics**: First described in *Ann. Mus. Congo, Zool.*, Vol. 2, p. 23, pl. 17.

**ansorgii**: after discoverer of the species, W. J. Ansorge.

**Description**: Sexual differentiation: Male usually more brightly colored with stronger, longer soft rays of dorsal and anal fins, and usually somewhat larger. Elongate, roundheaded species. Most colorful of the climbing

*Ctenopoma ansorgii* (BOULENGER, 1912)

| | | | | | |
|---|---|---|---|---|---|
| 8/7 cm | 24/26° C | I/II | H2 | Z2/3 | A 2 |
| D XVII–XVIII/7 | | A X–XI/7 | | | mLR 28–30 |

perches besides *Ctenopoma damasi.* During courtship and threatening posture, male is glistening green with 5 to 6 bold black transverse bands that extend into the dorsal and anal fins. The intervals between these bands are often colored orange. Older fish are often light brown without transverse bands.

**Distribution**: Found in the Chiloango River near Landana (48 miles north of the mouth of the Congo) and known at Stanley Pool (Poll, 1959). Reports of finding this fish in South Cameroon were apparently based upon erroneous information (Gartner, 1983). First introduced to Germany in 1955 or, according to some, 1958.

**Maintenance**: Very peaceful

*Ctenopoma ansorgii.* Photo by the author.

*Ctenopoma ansorgii.* Photo by the author.

fish that can be kept in a well-planted community tank that offers refuges, if the other fish don't harass them. Twilight fish that often stay in hiding. Best kept in well-planted, not too bright aquarium with the same species.

They require water that is soft and neutral or slightly acidic. Prepare with peat. Also can be kept in moderately hard water.

The diet consists particularly of aquatic live foods and fly larvae. Dry feed is inadequate as a long-term diet.

**Breeding**: Darkened tank of at least 7½-gallon capacity. In pairs. Feed with fly larvae (maggots). Peat bottom. Hiding place for female. Floating ferns (*Salvinia*) in darkest corner as support for the bubblenest. Do not disturb! Soft water, pH about 6. Twilight spawners, patriarchal brood. Remove female after the spawning phase.

Up to 600 crystal-clear floating eggs per spawning phase. Fry hatch as early as 24 hours later, and are free-swimming after another three days. Rotifers or paramecia as first food for three or four days, then freshly hatched *Artemia* nauplii. Fish that are even half an inch long are colorful.

## *Ctenopoma argentoventer* (Schreitmuller and Ahl, 1922)

SILVER-BELLIED *CTENOPOMA*

**Systematics**: First described in *Blaetter fuer Aquarien und Terrarienkunde*, p. 265. Often attributed to Ahl, *in* Schreitmuller and Ahl.

**argentoventer** Latin: with silvery abdomen.

*Ctenopoma argentoventer* (SCHREITMÜLLER und AHL, 1922)

| | | | | | |
|---|---|---|---|---|---|
| ca. 15 cm | 24/26° C | III | H1 | Z2/3 | A 3 |
| D XVI/10 | | A IX/10 | | | mLR 26 |

**Synonym** (invalid description): *Anabas africanus* (Vetterlein 1914).

**Description**: Sexual differentiation: Moderately large males have two yellowish stripes. One runs from the spiny part of the dorsal fin to the anal region, and the other arcs from the rear of the eye rim to the nape of the neck. Also, the male has spinous areas.

Young have silvery abdomen. Later, uniformly dark olive brown. Almost black in contentment and excitement. Black spot with light yellow margin at root of tail fades with age. Body scales with dark margins.

**Distribution**: Niger delta. First introduced by W. Kuntzschmann in 1912.

**Maintenance**: In community tanks with several others of same species when possible. Large tank with sufficient hiding spots. Not too brightly illuminated. Robust live foods, including meat bits and flake feed.

**Breeding**: Previously bred in home aquarium. No brood care.Young should hatch in 48 hours if properly kept, and swim free in another two days.

**Comments**: A cross between *Ctenopoma argentoventer* and *Anabas testudineus* was successful at the Frankfurt Zoo in 1919 (Arnold and Ahl, 1936). The species is not identical with *Ctenopoma kingsleyae*.

## *Ctenopoma brunneum* (Ahl, 1927)

**Systematics**: First described in "New African Fish of the *Anabantidae* and Cyprinodontidae families," in *Sitzungsber. Ges. naturforsch. Fr.* Berlin, p. 76. 1927.

**Description**: The largest of six specimens measured 3.2 inches in total length. The species is known only from preserved specimens, but is mentioned here only for the sake of completeness. Possibly a synonym of *C. nanum*.

*Ctenopoma brunneum* (AHL, 1927)

| | | |
|---|---|---|
| D XV/8-9 | A VIII/8-9 | mLR 26-27 |

## *Ctenopoma caudomaculatum* (Ahl, 1927)

SPOT-TAILED *CTENOPOMA*

**Systematics**: First described in "New African fish of the Anabatidae and Cyprinodontidae families," in *Sitzungsber. Ges. naturforsch. Fr.* Berlin, p. 77. 1927.

**caudomaculatum** Latin: with a spot on the tail.

**Description**: The species was described from a 3.4-inch long specimen. Coloration of live fish unknown. Color (in the specimen preserved in alcohol) was dark brown with a large black spot at the root of the caudal fin. Possibly a synonym of *C. petherici*.

*Ctenopoma caudomaculatum* (AHL, 1927)

| D XVII/10 | A VIII/11 | mLR 26 |
|---|---|---|

## *Ctenopoma congicum* Boulenger, 1887

CONGO *CTENOPOMA*

**Systematics**: First described in *Ann. Mag. Nat. Hist.* (5) XIX, p. 148.

**congicum**: refers to geographical origin.

**Description**: Relatively elongated climbing perch, slender and with rounder snout than *Ctenoponum fasciolatum*. Distinguished from *Ctenopomum nanum* by smaller head and by

*Ctenopoma congicum* male. Photo by the author.

*Ctenopoma congicum* BOULENGER, 1887

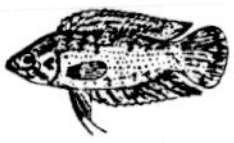

| 8,5/6 cm | 24/26° C | I/II | H1 | Z2 | A 3 |
|---|---|---|---|---|---|
| D XVI-XVII/8-9 | | A IX-XI/9-11 | | | mLR 26-28 |

dusky and light spots on the vertical fins. Yellowish to dark brown coloration, often similar to *C. fasciolatum* because of its wavy transverse pattern.

**Distribution**: Coastal area of equatorial West Africa and Ubangi, in part in common with *C. ansorgii*. First introduced presumably in 1953.

**Maintenance**: Peaceful fish that can be kept in not too bright community tanks. Water requirements less exacting than for *C. ansorgii*. Eats live food and flakes.

**Breeding**: Bubblenest builder. Set up breeding tank as for *C. ansorgii*. Fry hatch in about 24 to 30 hours, and swim free after another two or three days.

*Ctenopoma congicum* female. Photo by the author.

*Ctenopoma congicum* male. Photo by the author.

## *Ctenopoma ctenotis* (Boulenger, 1920)

COMB *CTENOPOMA*

**Systematics**: First described in "On some new fishes from near the west coast of Lake Tanganyika." *Proc. Zool. Soc. London*, p. 399.

***ctenotis:*** from Ktenos (Greek) - Comb.

**Description**: Closely related to *C. nanum*. Brownish, occasionally with faint transverse bands.

**Distribution**: Habitats reported from very different areas – upper Zambesi, Zambia, western Zaire. No live imports yet.

*Ctenopoma ctenotis* (BOULENGER, 1920)

| | | |
|---|---|---|
| D XV-XVII/8-10 | A IX-X/7-8 | mLR 27-29 |

## *Ctenopoma damasi* (Poll, 1939)

PEARL *CTENOPOMA*

**Systematics**: First described in "Fish.: Exploration of Albert National Park," Mission H. Damas (1935-1936). *Inst. des Parcs nationaux du Congo Belge.* Fasc. (Bruxelles), 1–73. Sometimes credited to Poll and Damas.

**damasi:** after H. Damas.

**Description**: Sexual differentiation: Pelvic fins of grown male distinctly longer, reaching into the anal fin when folded back. In the female, they reach only to the anus. Bright coloration seen in courting and brooding males also

*Ctenopoma damasi* male. Photo by the author.

*Ctenopoma damasi* (POLL, 1939)

| | | | | | |
|---|---|---|---|---|---|
| 7/6 cm | 26/27° C | II | H1 | Z2 | A3 |
| D (XIV-)XVI-XVIII(-XIX)/(6-)7-8(-9) | | A (IX-)X-XII/(6-)7-8(-9) | | mLR (26-)27-29(-30) | |

occurs in females in aggressive mood.

When in color: body and fins bluish-black with many bright blue spots. Pelvic fins, as well as pectoral and throat regions are uniformly blue. Females usually uniformly gray-brown like the non-territorial males.

**Distribution**: Zaire and Uganda on both sides of Lake Edward and in its vicinity. In small, turbid, heavily weeded and often very oxygen-poor pools. They avoid open water. Occasionally in communities with *C. muriei.* First introduced in 1968 by H. M. Peters and S. Berns, University of Tuebingen.

**Maintenance**: If possible in not too bright a tank with two females and one male. Floating *Ceratopteris*. Several hiding spots on the bottom. Thin peat layer over gravel. Shy fish which stay at the bottom often. Water soft and slightly acidic. Prefers coarse pond food, white fly larvae (maggots), *Notonecta glauca* (backswimmers) and smaller rainworms. Also accept dry food and meat bits as substitutes.

**Breeding**: Breeding tank as above. Males build compact, sturdy bubblenests. Spawning in the afternoon. Sensitive to disturbance. Patriarchal family. After the spawning phase, the male watches his nest, usually from the bottom. Floating eggs very small (diameter scarcely 0.8mm) and transparent. Young hatch at 80.6°F in 36 hours. Two days after hatching, they eat infusoria, and, in another 48 hours, freshly hatched brine shrimp nauplii. As early as the tenth day after hatching, they can be seen breathing with their labyrinth organs.

*Ctenopoma fasciolatum.* Photo by B. Kahl.

*Ctenopoma fasciolatum* (BOULENGER, 1899)

| | | | | | |
|---|---|---|---|---|---|
| 8,5/7 cm | 24/26° C | I/II | H1 | Z1 | A 2/3 |
| D XVI/8-9 | | A X/9-11 | | | mLR 27-28 |

*Ctenopoma fasciolatum* spawning. Photo by the author.

## *Ctenopoma fasciolatum* (Boulenger, 1899)

BANDED *CTENOPOMA*

**Systematics**: First described in "Description of a new osphromenoid fish from the Congo," in *Ann. Mag. Nat. Hist.* (7)III, p. 242.

**fasciolatum** (Latin): with narrow stripes or streaks.

**Description**: Sexual differentiation: Dorsal and anal fins strongly produced (i.e., clearly lengthened to a point). Male's ventral fins longer, often blue, unpaired fins with markings. About seven irregular blue-gray transverse bands on the flanks.

**Distribution**: Congo area in clear, lushly vegetated bank zones. First introduced as three specimens, July, 1912, by Siggelkow, Hamburg.

**Maintenance**: Active during the day. Peaceful and rather easily satisfied. Suitable for community tank, but needs many plants to provide cover. Feeding is not difficult, all food accepted.

**Breeding**: Egg-laden females can be recognized by their rounded, light-colored abdomen.

*Ctenopoma fasciolatum* spawning. Photo by the author.

*Ctenopoma fasciolatum* spawning. Photo by the author.

Males are bubblenest builders. Floating plants to support nest. Breeding tank not too bright. Patriarchal family. Remove females after spawning. Very productive. Young hatch after about 32 hours. They need infursoria first, then *Artemia* nauplii after four days.

## *Ctenopoma kingsleyae* **Günther, 1896**

KINGSLEY'S *CTENOPOMA*

**Systematics**: First described in *Ann. Mag. Nat. Hist.* (6), XVII, p. 270.

**kingsleyae:** from Mary Henrietta Kingsley (1862-1900), an English explorer and writer who travelled mostly in West Africa. *C. kingsleyae* presumably refers only to a southern variety of the previously described *C. petherici.* In that case, *C. kingsleyae* would be a synonym.

**Description**: Sexual differentiation: Females clearly larger than males of the same age, and somewhat more thick-set or dumpier. The male's spine areas are a definite distinguishing characteristic. Body strongly built, color gray, brown or dusky. Dark rims on scales. Throat and chest

*Ctenopoma kingsleyae* male. Photo by B. Kahl.

*Ctenopoma kingsleyae* GÜNTHER, 1896

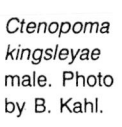

| | | | | | |
|---|---|---|---|---|---|
| 24,5 cm | 25/28° C | III | H1 | Z3 | A 2/3 |
| D XVI-XVIII/8-12 | | A VIII-X/9-12 | | | mLR 25-29 |

lighter, with a large shiny scale under the eye. Dark blotch in front of the caudal root often indistinct unless fright causes it to lighten and become more distinct.

**Distribution**: Humid and arid savannas of the West African nations from Senegal to Cameroon and Gabon. Slowly flowing rivers and lakes. Economic value in many places. First introduced in 1933.

**Maintenance**: A robust fish which always moves, but not erratically. Too large for indiscriminate community living, but very peaceful even toward much smaller fishes, as long as their size doesn't make them suitable for eating. Sometimes somewhat nervous or timid. Tail-spot climbing perch usually remain smaller than given in the data band above. However, their size still requires at least a 25-gallon tank, bigger if possible. Vegetation cover for hiding, but also adequate swimming room. Tank should not be too bright. Not territorial, so best in communities with their own kind. Diet and water requirements are modest, but still need sufficient energy-rich food– rainworms, flour beetle (weevil) larvae, tuna fish, fat-free bits of cooked ham, trout chow, feed tablets.

Long-lived – up to 14 years or longer.

**Breeding**: No brood care. Mating begins with a peculiar nodding accompanied by a clicking sound. Each spawning act produces 800-1000 eggs, and each spawning period produces 20,000 eggs, which make their way to the surface, from where they have to be scooped off. Young hatch in 24 hours at 84.2°F, in two days at 73.4°F (Ostermöller). The young, which swim free in about three days, take *Artemia* nauplii immediately.

*Ctenopoma maculatum* THOMINOT, 1886

| | | | | | |
|---|---|---|---|---|---|
| ca. 20 cm | 26° C | III | H1 | Z? | A 3 |

| | | |
|---|---|---|
| D XIV-XVI/9-11 | A VII-IX/9-11 | mLR 26-29 |

## *Ctenopoma maculatum* Thominot, 1886

SPOTTED *CTENOPOMA*

**Systematics**: First described in *Bull. Soc. Philom.* (7), p. 158.

**Synonyms**: *Anabas pleurostigma, Ctenopoma weeksii, C. multifasciata.*

**maculatum:** - spotted

**Description**: Sexual differentiation: Spine areas on males. Body build almost precisely between *petherici* and *C. oxyrhynchum.* Uniformly dark brown with large black spot in the middle of the flanks. Young have yellow-brown markings.

**Distribution**: South Cameroon (Nyong, Dja, Kienke or Kribi Rivers), Gabon, Congo; hidden in thickly overgrown bank zones of small flowing waters. First introduced (1 specimen) in 1976 by Linke, Berlin.

**Maintenance**: No special water requirements, despite its coming from soft water areas. Large tank with good hiding places along the sides and swimming space in the middle. Keep in communities only with sufficiently large tank-mates. Linke described the fish as unaggressive, but the same one developed into a regular bully when housed with the distinctly larger *C. petherici.* Eats all energy-rich live foods, especially earthworms. Also takes dry food.

## *Ctenopoma multispinis* Peters, 1844

MANY-SPINED *CTENOPOMA*

**Systematics**: First described in *Mon. ber. Akad. Berlin*, p. 34.

**multispinis** (Latin): many-spined, often erroneously *multispinnis* or *multispine.*

**Synonyms**: *Spirobranchus smithii, Anabas rhodesianus, Anabas vernayi.*

**Description**: Sexual differentiation: Anterior spinous areas of male easily recognizable even on living fish. Short pelvic fins which, when laid back, do not reach the base of the anal fin. Large scales, powerful (spiny) hard rays. Olive-brown to gray-green coloration, upper parts darker. Often with darker spots in soft rayed part of dorsal fin.

**Distribution**: In almost all southern African nations southward to Zululand, in extreme northeastern South Africa (according to Dr. P. Skelton, Albany Museum, Grahamstown). Chiefly in swampy areas and flood lands. Ecologically similar to *Anabas testudineus.* First introduced in 1935 (only one specimen). In April, 1972, D. Schaller imported six fish, which W. Foersch was able to breed in September, 1975.

**Maintenance**: Get along together, even with other species.

*Ctenopoma multispinis* PETERS, 1844

| D XVI-XIX/8-10 | A VIII-X/8-10 | mLR 31-35 |
|---|---|---|

Due to their size of about 14 cm total length (about 6″) not a prey fish. Keep in roomy tanks. Provide hiding spots in roots, Java moss, but also enough free swimming area. Cover tanks well! No requirements as to water quality or diet. Takes all coarser foods.

**Breeding**: No brood care. Spawning can be triggered by feeding. Foersch reports his fish (a large female and a distinctly smaller male) spawned after receiving 60-70 large flies for several days.

**Comments:** The multispined climbing perch is, like the quite similarly built *Anabas*, adapted to the periodic dry periods of its native waters. It can survive in the bottom of dried-up water bodies. Occasionally seen migrating overland. The earlier belief that the species is a mouthbrooder was based upon an error (Peters, 1971). A form from Angola considered here to be a subspecies is occasionally considered to be a full species (*C. machadoi*), but it lacks the spots on the dorsal fin.

## *Ctenopoma muriei* (Boulenger, 1906)

NILE *CTENOPOMA.*

**Systematics**: First described in *Ann. Mag. Nat. Hist.* (7) XVIII, p. 348.

**Synonym**: *Anabas houyi, Anabas muriei ocellifer* (subspecies ?)

**Description**: Sexually mature at 4 months. Male 1.8 inches, female 2.2 inches. In the wild, captured specimens seldom more than 3.2 inches total length. Sexual differentiation: Females more robust, males with spine area.

Beige-brown, on flanks indistinct gray spots. Gray, pale rimmed spot on root of tail.

**Distribution**: Native to the drainage area of the White Nile as far as Lake Chad basin and Lake Edward in small swampy lakes or stagnating and slowly flowing water. First introduced in 1968 by S. Berns and H. M. Peters, Tuebingen.

**Maintenance**: Large, not too bright tanks. Active, so need sufficient swimming space. Water not too hard. Accept live foods of all kinds and, after getting used to it, dry foods.

**Breeding**: Tanks as above. Introduce pairs or several together. Two or three males often pursue one female. Mating predominantly between 9 p.m. and 12 p.m. No brood care. Often 2,000 eggs per spawning phase.

At 80.6°F, young hatch in 22 to 26 hours and swim free in about four days.

*Ctenopoma muriei* (BOULENGER, 1906)

| | | | | | |
|---|---|---|---|---|---|
| ca. 6,5/9,7 cm | 24/26° C | III | H1 | Z2 | A 3 |
| D XIV-XVI/7-10 | | A VIII-XI/(7-)8-11 | | | mLR (24)25-28 |

*Ctenopoma multispinis*, wild specimen. Photo by Pierre Brichard, the collector of this species in the Congo River area of Africa.

# *Ctenopoma nanum* (Günther, 1896)

DWARF *CTENOPOMA*

**Systematics**: First described in *Ann. Mag. Nat. Hist.* (6) XVII, p. 269.

**nanus** (Latin): dwarf.

**Description.** Sexual differentiation: Male larger, with pointed dorsal and anal fins in their rearward extension. Vertical fins, unlike *C. fasciolatum* and *C. congicum*, without spots. Body with 6 to 8 transverse bands. In full color, male dark blue, almost black. Female light ocher in courtship and mating coloration. Transverse bands broken by a light longitudinal stripe.

**Distribution**: South Cameroon, Gabon, Congo basin and large areas of Angola in very small, shady flowing waters of the rain forest. D. Schaller caught, in all

*Ctenopoma nanum* GÜNTHER, 1896

| | | | | | |
|---|---|---|---|---|---|
| 7,5/6,5 cm | 24/25° C | I/II | H1 | Z2 | A 3 |
| D XV-XVIII/7-10 | | A VII-X/9-11 | | | mLR 25-30 |

An immature specimen of *Ctenopoma nanum*. Photo by Dr. Herbert R. Axelrod.

probability, two fish of this species in 1972 in a flood area of the Zambesi about 18 miles northwest of Beira; with them, he also caught *C. multispinis*, *Protopterus annectens*, *Nothobranchus rachovii*, an *Aplocheilichthys* species, *Clarias* spp., and two different *Alestes* spp. The distribution of this species here is, on one hand, indication of its wide distribution, and on the other hand, just how inadequate the distribution of the individual labyrinth species in Africa is known, even today. First introduction was in 1933.

**Maintenance**: Relatively without any problems. Well planted tank. Also suitable for the community tank. Moderately hard water, better if soft. Neutral or slightly acidic. Live foods are preferred, but also accepts dry food.

**Breeding**: By pairs in 7 1/2- to 12 1/2-gallon tanks. Keep dim, with hiding spots and swimming area. Don't disturb! Start the young on fly larvae. Males build bubblenests. Young hatch in 24 hours. Free-swimming in three days. First food: rotifers or *Paramecium* and, in another three days, *Artemia* nauplii.

**Comments**: This species is apparently split into subspecies. Variants (other species ?) have been reported from Gabon (Gartner, 1983) as well as from Angola (Poll, 1967).

*Ctenopoma nigropannosum* REICHENOW, 1875

| | | | | | |
|---|---|---|---|---|---|
| 17 cm | 25° C | III | H2 | Z3? | A 3 |
| D XIX-XX/9-10 | | A IX-XI/9-10 | | | mLR 30-33 |

## *Ctenopoma nigropannosum* Reichenow, 1875

TWO-SPOTTED *CTENOPOMA*.

**Systematics**: First described in *Sitzungsber. Ges. naturforsch. Fr.*, Berlin, p. 147.

**nigropannosum** (Latin): with dark patches, blotches at root of tail on both sides.

**Synonym**: *Ctenopoma gabonense*.

**Description.** Sexual differentiation: Males recognizable only by their anterior spine areas. Elongated fish with somewhat pointed head. Yellow-brown with only transient irregular transverse bands. Small spots on hind half of body. Deep black spot at root of tail.

**Distribution**: Region of Congo mouth according to Boulenger (1916) in swamps and creeks. First introduced in 1933.

**Maintenance**: Large tanks with hiding spots on the sides and with a lot of swimming room. Keep only with its own kind. Lively fish which likes to jump. Also eats plants, according to Arnold and Ahl.

**Breeding**: No brood care. Breeding in captivity not yet successful.

## *Ctenopoma ocellatum* Pellegrin, 1899

CHOCOLATE BUSHFISH.

**Systematics**: *Bull. Mus. Paris*, p. 359.

**ocellatum** (Latin): provided with an eyespot.

**Synonyms**: *Anabas weeksii, Ctenopoma denticulatum.*

**Description:** Sexual differentiation: eye-spot of male larger. Male has spine areas. Female higher-backed. Similar in body build and behavior to the higher-backed *C. acutirostre* and *C. oxyrhynchum*, which are occasionally confused with it.

Striking black, pale-rimmed eye-spot or blotch (ocellus) at the root of the tail. Irregular wavy transverse bands on the body.

**Distribution**: The species is native to the whole lower Congo basin, often along with *C. acutirostre*. First introduced in 1956.

**Maintenance**: Keep only with quiet, not too small fish. Set up tank as for *C. acutirostre*. The diet described there, too, is appropriate for *C. ocellatum.*

**Breeding**: No breeding yet reported.

*Ctenopoma ocellatum* PELLEGRIN, 1899

| | | | | | |
|---|---|---|---|---|---|
| ca. 14 cm | 26° C | II/III | H2 | Z3 | A 3 |
| D XVI-XVIII/9-12 | | A IX-X/10-12 | | | mLR 26-28 |

*Ctenopoma ocellatum*. Photo by W. Foersch.

*Ctenopoma ocellatum*, juvenile. Photo by Dr. Herbert R. Axelrod of a specimen he collected in Zaire (Congo) in 1969.

*Ctenopoma oxyrhynchum* (BOULENGER, 1902)

| | | | | | |
|---|---|---|---|---|---|
| 10 cm | 24/26° C | I/III | H1 | Z2 | A 2 |
| D XV/10 | | A VIII/10 | | | mLR 28 |

*Ctenopoma oxyrhynchum*. Photo by B. Kahl.

# *Ctenopoma oxyrhynchum* (Boulenger, 1902)

MOTTLED *CTENOPOMA*.

**Systematics**: First described in *Ann. Mus. Congo Zool.*, II, pg 52.

**oxyrhynchum** (Greek): sharp-snouted, with pointed mouth.

**Description**: Female usually somewhat more robust. Only the spine areas of the males are unequivocal sexual differences. Pointed snout and relatively high-backed. Very variable coloration, light ocher to dark brown variegated or piebald, usually with black spot in the middle of the body. Black band from tip of snout to eye, forming an arc behind the eye and running to the base of the dorsal fin. Another band begins somewhat lower on the rear rim of the eye and bends distinctly down to the lower margin of the gill cover.

**Distribution**: Lower Congo basin around Lake Stanley and Ubangi (near Banzyville), along with *C. pellegrini.* First introduced in 1952 into Hamburg.

**Maintenance**: Relatively peaceful fish that sees smaller tank-mates as food. Good for a

community tank that contains equally large tank-mates. Lives well, too, with *C. acutirostre.* Accepts all kinds of not too small live food and supplemental prepared foods, as well as small and moderately large earthworms.

**Breeding**: Not too small a tank (from 20 gallons up). Introduce by pairs. Root hideouts along sides, not too bright. Thin layer of peat on bottom. No brood care. Releases eggs right on the bottom at night. After a short chase, a hasty two-second spawning act. The eggs float upward. Up to 2,000 eggs can be released each spawning phase.

The young hatch after about 24 hours and after another three days are free-swimming. Sensitive to light! Soon eat *Artemia* (brine shrimp) nauplii.

## *Ctenopoma pellegrini* (Boulenger, 1902)

PELLEGRIN'S *CTENOPOMA.*

**Systematics:** First described in Ann. Mus. Congo 2(1), p.51

**pellegrini:** after the French ichthyologist Jacques Pellegrin.

**Description**: Boulenger reports a total length of 4.1 inches. Elongated fish with rounded snout and relatively large mouth. Body olive color, darker above, indistinct stripe marking anteriorly.

**Distribution**: Upper Ubangi near Banzyville on the northern border of Zaire, in association with *C. oxyrhynchum.*

**Maintenance**: No information yet for aquarium.

**Miscellaneous**: Belongs to the lively slender forms in which there is no brood care, such as *C. multispinis* and *C. nigropannosum.* To be cared for, presumably, as for these two species.

## *Ctenopoma petherici* Günther, 1864

PETHERICK'S *CTENOPOMA.*

**Systematics**: First described in *Ann. Mag. Nat. Hist.* (3) XIII, p. 211.

**petherici:** after the collector J. Petherick.

There are many indications that *C. kingsleyae* is only a geographical variant of this species.

**Description**: Sexual differentiation: Female distinctly larger and somewhat squatter or more thickly-set than males of the

*Ctenopoma pellegrini* (BOULENGER, 1902)

| | | |
|---|---|---|
| D XVIII-XIX/10-11 | A VII/10 | mLR 33-34 |

*Ctenopoma petherici* GÜNTHER, 1864

| | | | | | |
|---|---|---|---|---|---|
| 19 cm | 25/28° C | III | H1 | Z3 | A 4 |

| | | |
|---|---|---|
| D XVII-XIX/8-11 | A VIII-XI/9-11 | mLR 25-30 |

same age. Spine areas of male are most reliable difference. Powerful body. Gray, brown or blackish coloration.

**Distribution**: Arid savannas of northern Africa on the upper Niger, in the Chad region, on the upper Benue as well as on the White Nile.

**Maintenance**: In all probability will not differ essentially, if at all, from *C. kingsleyae* in maintenance and breeding.

## Genus *Sandelia* Castelnau, 1861

CAPE LABYRINTH FISHES

**Number of Species**: 3

**Distribution**: Only in the extreme south of South Africa in the coastal areas between Capetown and East London.

**Systematics**: *Sandelia* refers to a Bantu chief of the Gaika tribe, Sandeli (1820-1878).

**Synonym**: *Spirobranchus* was often used previously.

**Comments**: Cape labyrinth fish differ from the climbing perches or bush fish by their essentially more weakly spined gill cover and a smaller, less efficient labyrinth organ. The reduction of the labyrinth organ is explainable by the occurrence of the Cape labyrinth fish in cooler, oxygen-richer flowing waters. That also is associated with a different spawning behavior.

## *Sandelia bainsii* Castelnau, 1861

BAINS CAPE ANABANTOID.

**Systematics**: First described in *Mem. Poiss. Afr. Austr.*, p. 37

**bainsii:** in honor of the geologist A. G. Bain.

**Synonym**: *Ctenopoma microlepidotum*

**Description**: Secondary sexual

*Sandelia bainsii* CASTELNAU, 1861

| | | | | | |
|---|---|---|---|---|---|
| 19/21 cm | 20° C | III | H2 | Z3 | A 3 |
| D XV-XVII/9-10 | | A VII-VIII/9-10 | | | mLR 33-35 |

*Sandelia bainsii.* Photo by W. Foersch.

characteristics unknown. Robust fish with large mouth. According to Schaller, a pointed-head and a more blunt-headed form. Body dark gray-green, occasionally olive green scales on flanks. Darker than *S. capensis*, with pointed ends to dorsal and anal fins. Indistinct stripes from lower margin of eye to corner of anterior gill covers.

**Distribution**: Dispersed in rivers on southern tip of Africa near the cities of East London, King William Town, and Grahamstown. Earlier finds around Capetown and Port Elizabeth no longer corroborated now. Schaller caught the species in very rapidly flowing and relatively cold "trout" waters. See *S. capensis*. First introduced in 1973 by Dietrich Schaller of Munich.

**Maintenance**: Extraordinarily aggressive toward its own kind and others. Species tank with many hiding spots. Filter or aeration. Not yet bred in captivity.

## *Sandelia capensis* (Cuvier and Valenciennes, 1831)

CAPE ANABANTOID.

**Systematics**: First described in *Hist. Nat. poiss.* VII, p. 392, plate cc.

**capensis**: from Cape Colony or Cape Province, origin of the species.

**Description**: Sexual differences: Male essentially darker than female during spawning. Large-headed species less elongated than *S. bainsii* and lighter. Dorsal and anal fins rounded off posteriorly. Three dark stripes from rear margin of eye radiate divergently to anterior gill cover.

**Distribution**: In rivers, ponds, streams and lakes of southwestern Cape Colony. First introduced in 1973 by Schaller. He captured them near Port Elizabeth (suburbs, about 6 miles from the center of the city) in extremely acid, partially eutrophic ("tea") water. The water was warmer and not so fast-flowing as at the sites where *S. bainsii* was found.

**Maintenance**: Not too suitable for community living, although hardly aggressive toward others of its own species. Large tank. Provide hiding spots. Unpretentious in respect to water quality and diet.

**Breeding**: I only have field observations (Jubb, 1967) for reference which are such that they should be given here. Can reproduce as early as the first year (from 2 inches length on). Mating in spring and early summer at shallow, poorly flowing spots. No nest building. Spawn sinks to

*Sandelia capensis* (CUVIER und VALENCIENNES, 1831)

| | | | | | |
|---|---|---|---|---|---|
| 20/22 cm | 22/25° C | III | H2 | Z3? | A 3 |
| D XII-XIV/8-10 | | A VI-VII/8-11 | | | mLR 26-30 |

*Sandelia vicina* (BOULENGER, 1916)

D XIII-XV/8-9 A VIII-IX/8-9 mLR 27-29

bottom where it sticks to plants or stones. Males remain at the spawning place and watch the eggs. Young hatch at 75.2°F in 35 hours and are free-swimming on the third day.

## *Sandelia vicina* (Boulenger, 1916)

**Systematics**: First described in *Catalogue of the freshwater fishes of Africa*. London, p. 51–52.

**vicina** (Latin): neighboring, in the vicinity, presumably referring to the close relationship to *S. capensis*.

**Description**: Boulenger reports 4.7 inches as the longest total length. The describer differentiates *S. vicina* from *S. capensis* by the greater number of gill spines in the lower part of the gill arch (*vicina* 9–11, *capensis* 8–9). Coloration brownish, often spotted black. Characteristic black spots and stripes on dorsal fin.

**Distribution**: Small rivers in region of the South African seaport of Port Elizabeth. Possibly already extinct. No details for keeping in aquarium.

# THE LABYRINTH FISHES OF THE INDIAN SUBCONTINENT

**Subcontinent of India**–jungles, steppes, deserts, cultivated land, and wilderness. The varied landscape is associated with many species, to which particularly attractive aquarium fishes belong. I include Pakistan, India, Sri Lanka (Ceylon), Bangladesh and Burma as parts of the subcontinent of India. Geographically, Burma should be with "further" India or Indo-China. In regard to the zoogeography, especially the distribution of fish species, however, the situation is different. There are only a few differences between the fishes of the Indian subcontinent and those of Burma. On the other hand, the mountainous barriers between Burma and Thailand represent quite an important zoogeographic boundary. Only a few species occur on both sides of this boundary. Also, the number of genera that cross this boundary is not very large.

The typical labyrinth fish representatives of the Indian subcontinent are the *Colisa* species, the western threadfins, which are so superbly suited to keeping in the aquarium. The other labyrinth fishes are much less in evidence. Their distribution is limited to smaller areas, such as in the case for *Parasphaerichthys* or the *Malpulutta kretseri* species endemic to Sri Lanka, and the Ceylonese Macropode, *Belontia signata*. Seven labyrinth fish genera with eleven species are known from the Indian subcontinent region.

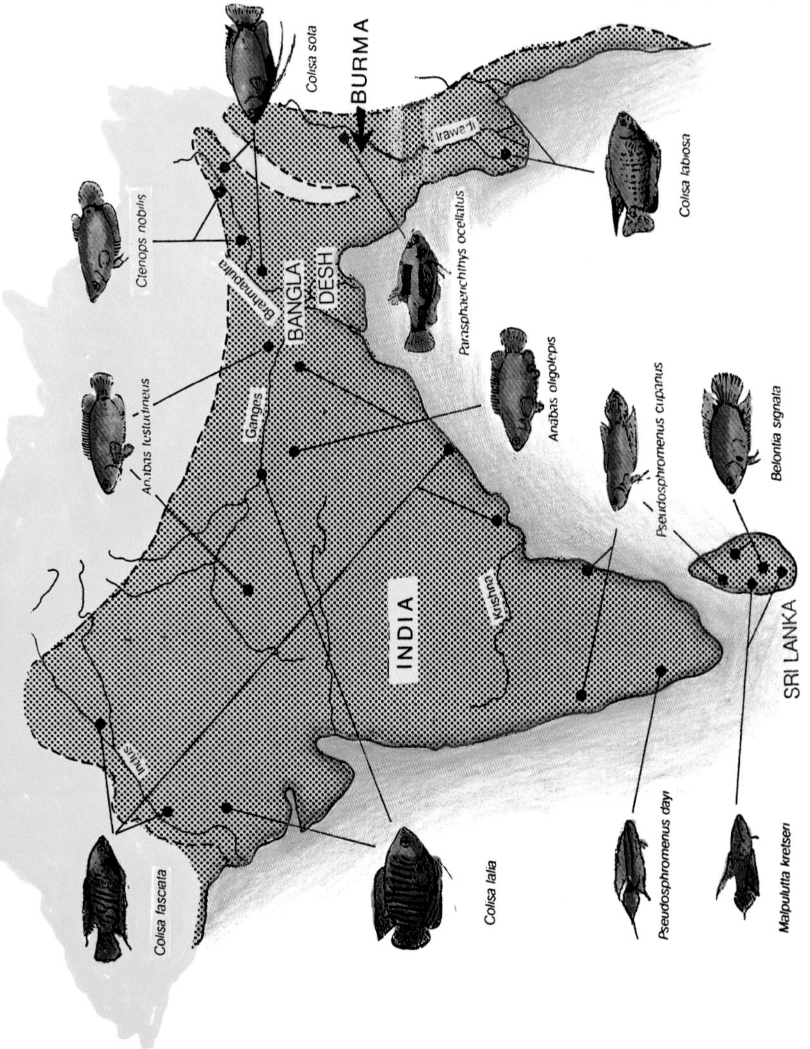


Distribution of labyrinth fishes on the Indian subcontinent.
The dashes (- - - - ) indicate the extent of the ranges. Drawn by J. Dittmar after a sketch by the author.

## Genus *Anabas* Cuvier, 1816

CLIMBING PERCHES (in the strict sense).

**Number of Species**: 2

**Systematics**: 1817 is generally given as the year of the first description of the genus, as noted in Cuvier's *Regne anim.* In fact, however, this work was already published by the end of 1816, so this year is the valid one (Jayaram).

**Anabas** (Greek): climber, ascender.

**Distribution**: Freshwater fish that occasionally goes into brackish waters. Ranges over all of Indian subcontinent, Malayan Archipelago, Indo-China, the Philippines, and also South China.

**Comments**: Ability to survive dry spells by encasing themselves in hardened mud at the bottom of dried-out bodies of water as in their overland migration.

The climbing fish are valued commercially throughout their range.

## *Anabas oligolepis* Bleeker, 1855

SCANT-SCALED CLIMBING PERCH.

**Systematics**: First described in *Nat. Tijdschr. Ned. Ind*, VII, p. 161.

**oligolepis** (Latin): with few scales. Bleeker reported 27 scales along the lateral line for the species, and 30 to 32 for *A. testudineus.*

The name was long a synonym for *A. testudineus*, but studies by Dutt and Rameseshaiah (1981) revealed, besides differences in the construction of the labyrinth organ, differences in chromosome count – *A. testudineus* has 48, and *A. oligolepis* has 46 chromosomes.

*A. macrocephalus* is a true synonym.

**Description**: Similar to *A. testudineus*, but deeper bodied (body height goes into standard length 2.5 to 2.9 times, but 3.1 to 3.5 in *A. testudineus*). Shorter pectoral fins than *A. testudineus*, longer snout, and lacks the black spot at the root of the tail. Size as in *A. testudineus.*

**Distribution**: Both *Anabas* species occur together in large areas of India, near Calcutta, Andhra Pradesh and Orissa. It's very questionable whether the species has ever been imported alive into Europe or the U.S.A. In keeping and breeding, it's probable that it hardly differs at all from *A. testudineus.*

## *Anabas testudineus* (Bloch, 1795)

CLIMBING PERCH.

**Systematics**: First described as *Anthias testudineus* in *Ausl. Fische VI*, p. 121, plate CCXXII.

**testudineus** (Latin): turtle-like, because of the hard scaly armor.

*Anabas oligolepis* BLEEKER, 1855

D XVII-XVIII/9-10 A IX-XI/8-12 mLR 21-29

*Anabas testudineus* (BLOCH, 1795)

| | | | | | |
|---|---|---|---|---|---|
| 18/23 cm | 24/28° C | III | H1/2 | Z2 | A 2/3 |

| | | |
|---|---|---|
| D XV-XVIIXVII-XIX/7-9 | A IX-XI/8-12 | mLR 26-32 |

The list of synonyms is long. The most frequently used ones are as follows:

*Perca scandens*; *Amphiprion testudineus*; *Lutjanus testudo*; *Sparus scandens*; *Cojus cobojius*; *Anabas spinosus*; *Anabas microcephalus*; *Anabas elongatus*.

**Description**. Sexual differentiation: Under the same living conditions, females distinctly larger than males. Abdominal outline is rounded in females, and straight in the more slender males. Adult males usually have diagonally arranged rows of dots on the flanks.

Elongated but also robust fish very widely built, especially in the head and anterior part of the body, snout rounded. Strong scales. Dark opercular spot and bright-rimmed dark blotch at root of tail, but fading with age.

Color generally gray, eyes reddish. Dark band running rearwards from mouth, with a less bold parallel stripe underneath.

**Distribution**: Commonly found in all of Southeast Asia from Pakistan to the Philippines, from Taiwan to Ceylon (Sri Lanka) and Timor. Its range is greater than that of any other labyrinth fish.

The common climbing perch is unpretentious and lives in all flowing and standing freshwater and brackish waters. Found more often in coastal flat land than further inland.

First introduced: About 1870, climbing fish were being kept in the London Aquarium.

**Maintenance**: Not difficult to keep in properly managed aquarium. Climbing perch sometimes eat plants and will pursue small fishes. Decorate with rocks and roots. Planting is a matter of luck. The fish need places to hide; they are shy and cautious, predominantly active at twilight.

Community tanks with equally large and robust fish (e.g., *Ctenopoma kingsleyae*) are quite feasible. Tolerate each other, since they are not territorial. Long-lived. I, personally, have been keeping three fish (one female, two males) now for several years in a 20-gallon tank without ever having had any problems.

Not fussy about water or food, but eats a lot. Accepts, besides dry flake food and pellets, also worms, meat and any kind of coarse pond food.

Cover the aquarium well! Recommended for specialists.

**Breeding**: Sexually mature at 4 to 6 inches. Climbing perch do not care for brood. Spawning is initiated by the males, usually in the evening or at night.

Light yellow floating eggs 0.3 to 0.39 inch in diameter. Young hatch after 24 to 36 hours and are free-swimming in another 48 hours. First bred in 1896 in the

*Anabas testudineus* in search of a new home. Photo by the author.

cement tanks of the P. Matte Institution (Berlin-Lankwitz), and in an aquarium by O. Schroeder (Hamburg) in 1909.

According to information from K. Schaller, *Anabas* spawn in the rice fields of Thailand almost regularly one to two days following heavy rainfall, after the storm-tossed waters have subsided and the water becomes clear again.

## Genus *Belontia* Myers, 1923

COMBTAILS.

**Number of species**: 2

**Systematics**: Characteristic of the genus *Belontia* is the construction of the pelvic fins. The first ray is split. Its end, in older fish, is drawn out into two more or less long threads.

**Belontia**: originated from the Palembang (Sumatra) designation "Belontja" for the Java combtail *B. hasselti.*

**Distribution**: One of the few labyrinth fish genera that is represented in South Asia as well as in Southeast Asia. The Ceylonese *Belontia* is endemic to Sri Lanka.

**Comments**: The young have a distinct black blotch at the base of the soft rayed dorsal fin which serves to pacify the adults. Older youngsters, too, show this blotch when they are attacked by stronger members of their species.

## *Belontia signata* (Günther, 1861)

COMBTAIL.

**Systematics**: First described as *Polyacanthus signatus* in *Catalogue of the fishes in the collection of the British Museum.*

**signata** (Latin): marked, characterized.

**Description.** Sexual differentiation: No unequivocal physical differences. Older males often have somewhat larger fins, especially longer rays in the caudal fin. Females usually somewhat stockier, broader bellies full of eggs when spawning.

*Belontia signata* (GÜNTHER, 1861)

| | | | | | |
|---|---|---|---|---|---|
| 15/13,5 cm | 24/28° C | I/II | H1 | Z2 | A 2 |

| | | |
|---|---|---|
| D XVI-XVIII/7-10 | A XIV-XVII/9-12 | mLR 29-32 |

*Belontia hasselti* juvenile. Photo by Aaron Norman.

Robust fish with reddish-brown ground color. Caudal fin rays lengthen with age. The skin between the rays of the dorsal, anal, and caudal fins, as well as their margins, glisten turquoise blue when the light strikes just right. Two distinct body builds:

1. Bullish, high-backed, not so intensively colored. No chest blotch. Rougher behavior: ***B. signata signata***.

2. Slenderer and more intense coloration. Partially reddish-brown body. Iridescent light blue scales on neck and underparts. Striking blue-black spot at base of pectoral fin: subspecies ***B. signata jonklaasi***.

These two subspecies are apparently related by means of intermediate forms.

**Distribution**: Endemic in Ceylon (present-day Sri Lanka). Lives hidden in small bodies of water, preferably in clear streams and rivulets. Likes to stay protected in bank zone among roots and water plants.

The following values are reported for native waters: temperature between 77 and 82.4°F, pH 6-6.5, hardness 0.2-0.65.

**Maintenance**: For communities, moderately large South American cichlids (*Cichlasoma* or *Geophagus*) are admirably suitable. Large tanks (5 feet and larger), however, are

necessary. Peaceful toward smaller tank-mates only as long as breeding fervor is absent, at which time even rivals of the same species will be fought. Then the lower-ranking fish have to be removed. The parents-to-be defend their territory very vigorously. They don't attack plants, but love hiding places. Relatively unpretentious as far as water and diet go. Omnivorous; eats dry flake food and pellets, worms, meat, flour weevils (or beetles) and coarse pond food.

**Breeding**: No problems when accomplished with suitable pair on varied diet (live food!). Best with introduction of pairs in well planted tank provided with roots and a capacity of at least 18 gallons; more is even better. Water hardness up to 12 degrees.

Typical bubblenest is not built. Floating eggs are gathered into one or more clumps (or rafts), cemented together with a salivary secretion, and preferably placed under floating leaves, then guarded by the male. The female occasionally also helps gather up and care for the brood. Normally, the females guard the peripheral part of the territory, defending it against any intruders. Parental families with tendency toward mouth-brooding.

Eggs turbid, rather large (diameter about 1.8 mm). At 82.4°F, young hatch after 28 to 32 hours. They are free-swimming 90 hours following release of eggs, immediately feeding on freshly hatched *Artemia* nauplii.

Rearing the young is no problem. The parents still guard the free-swimming young for several weeks, but without actively holding them together. The young don't school, but remain in their parents' territory, thus are still under their protection.

*Belontia signata* spawning. Photo by the author.

A male *Belontia signata* under a clump of eggs. Photo by the author.

**Colisa:** from kholisha - Native name for threadfins in western Assam.

**Subfamily**: Trichogasterinae

**Distribution:** Streams, ponds, flooded meadows and rice paddies near the large rivers of northern India, from the Indus in Pakistan to Rangoon in Burma.

**Comments**: Genus of labyrinth fishes with the most suitable members for keeping in aquariums, and which are lively, colorful, peaceful and unpretentious. In addition, their great number of complex behavioral aspects place them among the most interesting of aquarium fishes.

# Genus *Colisa* Cuvier and Valenciennes, 1831

**DWARF GOURAMIS.**

**Number of Species**: 4

**Systematics**: For a long time the western threadfins were grouped together with the eastern ones under the name of *Trichogaster* or *Trichopodus*. The division is, to be sure, fully justified, for the smaller *Colisa* species differ from the eastern threadfins in several distinct ways: their dorsal fin is about as long as the anal fin (much shorter, though, in *Trichogaster*), and the pelvic fin is reduced to a single thread-like process (in *Trichogaster*, also 2 or 3 smaller soft rays besides the thread). However, many other characteristics evidence the close relationship of these two genera.

Differences in the proportions of the species *Colisa fasciata, C. labiosa, C. lalia* and the cross *C. labiosa* x *C. lalia*. Drawing by W. Weiss after a draft by the author. GL = Total Length; KL = Head Length; KH = Greatest Body Depth.

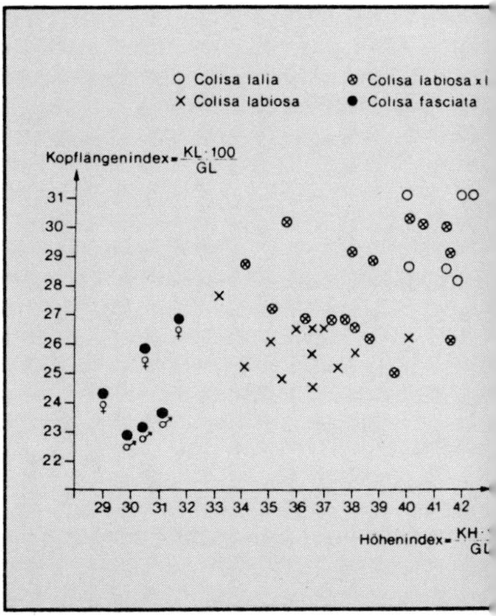

*Colisa fasciata* (BLOCH und SCHNEIDER, 1801)

| | | | | | |
|---|---|---|---|---|---|
| 12,7/10 cm | 25/28° C | I | H1/2 | Z1 | A 2 |
| D XV-XVII/9-14 | | A XV-XVIII/14-19 | | | mLR 29-31 |

A pair of Giant Gouramis, *Colisa fasciata,* under their nest. Photo by the author.

## *Colisa fasciata* (Bloch and Schneider, 1801)

GIANT GOURAMI, BANDED GOURAMI.

**Systematics**: First described in *Systema ichthyol*, 164, plate XXXVI as *Trichogaster fasciatus.* The species is also known by the following synonyms: *Trichopodus colisa*, *T. cotra*, *Colisa bejeus*, *C. ponteriana*, *C. vulgaris* and *Polyacanthus fasciatus.*

The fin formula matches that of *C. labiosa*, so for a long time that species was considered a geographical variant of *C. fasciata.* There are, however, unmistakable characteristics, so there should be no doubt as to the species status of both species. *C. fasciata* is distinctly more elongated than *C. labiosa.* Besides, *C. fasciata* males have pointed dorsal and anal fins (in *labiosa*, the anal fin is always rounded). Recent chromosome analyses (Manna and Prasad) evidenced unequivocal differences.

**fasciata** (Latin): banded.

**Description**: The size in the band refers to captured specimens. In aquarium tanks I have never seen males longer

*Colisa fasciata* spawning. Photo by Hans-Joachim Richter.

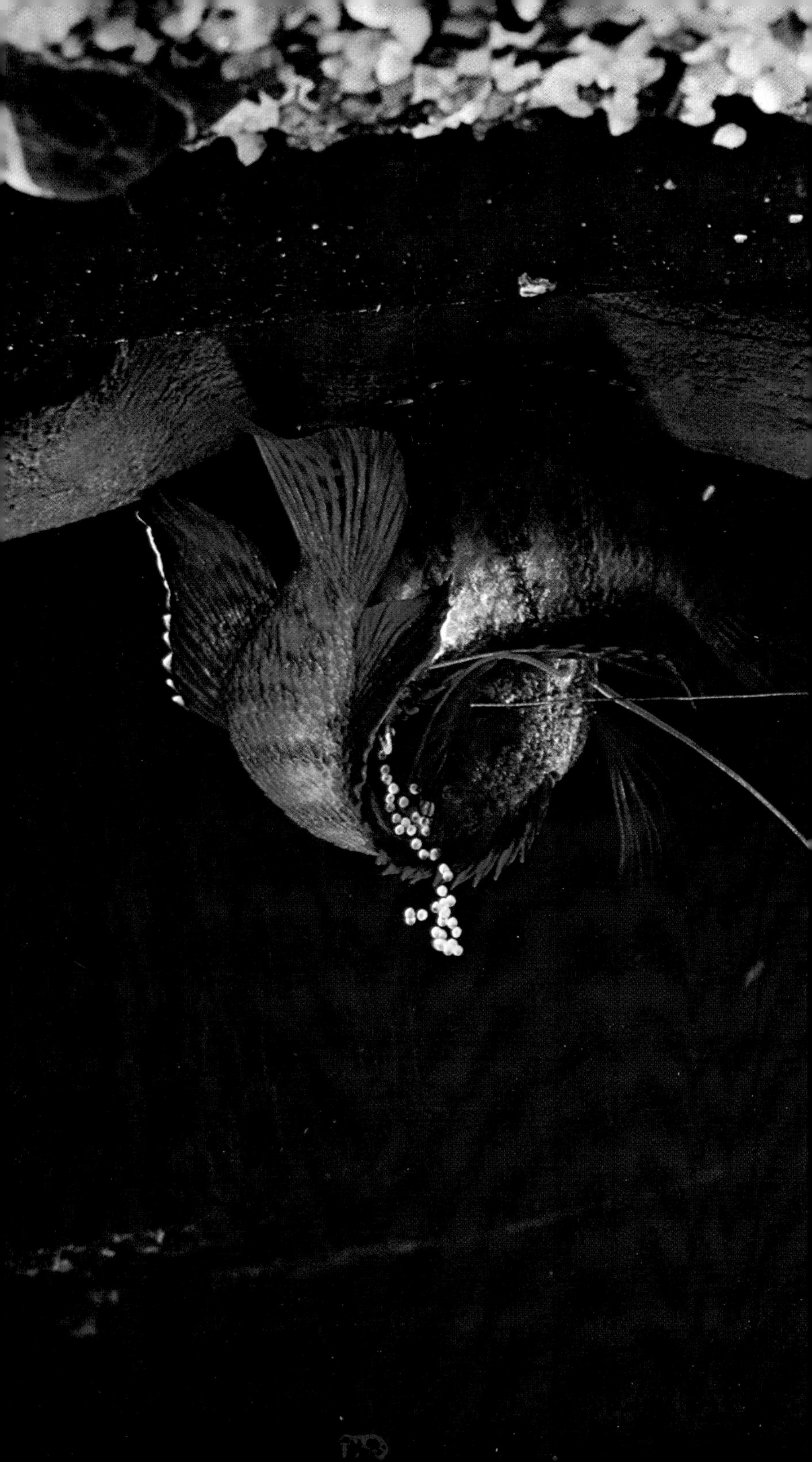

than 3.5 inches. Females are usually all under 2.8 inches.

Sexual differentiation: The males, which are longer, have pointed tips to their dorsal and anal fins; these fins are rounded in the females. When in full color, the males can be recognized at once.

*C. fasciata* are small-headed, elongated threadfins whose physical build differs significantly from that of *C. labiosa*. Their greatest body height often hardly exceeds the head height.

Characteristic of both sexes is a black-and-white chin strap which runs from one eye to the other. Otherwise, coloration is very variable. Males in full color have dark brownish-red ground color traversed by about 10 light-blue glistening diagonal bands. Chest and throat are blackish to blue. Anal fin usually shines blue with an orange-red margin. Eyes and pectoral fin threads in the male are red.

**Distribution**: Native to the lowlands on the Coromandel coast southward to the Krishna River, and northward to the Ganges delta, then further northeastward to all of Bangladesh, Nepal and Assam. Further distribution on the upper and presumably also on the middle Ganges, as well as in the region of the Indus lowlands in Punjab and Sind. The ecology coincides largely with that of *Colisa sota*.

Striped or banded gouramis are common in India, where, in many places, they are dried and eaten.

First brought to England by Captain Sipan in the 1880's. In 1897, Paul Matte (Berlin) imported 40 *C. fasciata* from Calcutta.

**Maintenance**: Excellent for the well-planted community tank. Peaceful, but males become rather aggressive during the spawning season.

No particular water or diet needs, but they are big eaters. Imported specimens occasionally infected by gill worms.

**Breeding**: To encourage good spawning, feed the females well with living mosquito larvae. Introduce by pairs into thickly planted 20-gallon tank.

Males build large bubblenests. Provide refuges for the female for she is often pursued. Mating occurs in the afternoon or evening, and can last over two hours. About 600 to 700 eggs are produced during each spawning phase. Young hatch after 24 hours, are free-swimming in another two days, when they need very small food (infusoria), and then, after about a week more, freshly hatched *Artemia*.

## *Colisa labiosa* (Day, 1878)

THICK-LIPPED GOURAMI.

**Systematics**: First described in *Fishes of India*, p. 374, plate LXXIX, Fig. 4 as *Trichogaster labiosus*.

**labiosa** (Latin): fully developed lips.

**Description.**: Sexual differentiation: Males larger, with pointed end of dorsal fin which can reach to the end of the tail fin.

A pair of Thick-lipped Gouramis, *Colisa labiosa.* Photo by B. Kahl.

*Colisa labiosa* (DAY, 1878)

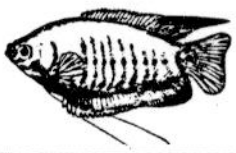

| | | | | | |
|---|---|---|---|---|---|
| 9/8 cm | 25/28° C | I | H1 | Z1 | A 1/2 |
| D XV-XVIII/8-10 | | A XVI-XVIII/17-20 | | | mLR 29-31 |

No confusion when in full color.

Built higher than *C. fasciata*, otherwise very similar to this species, but distinguished because even the male's anal fin is rounded. The thick lips for which it gets its name are not characteristic of the species, for they are also found in older *C. fasciata* and *C. lalia.*

Just as in *C. fasciata*, both sexes of *C. labiosa* also have a striking black-and-white chin band running from eye to eye. The full coloration, too, of the male is similar to that of *C. fasciata*, although the ground color of the body can become brownish-black during spawning. Pelvic fins and margin of anal fins yellowish or orange.

Females sometimes exhibit a dark band running from the eye to the root of the caudal fin; often, you can see the individual spots making up this band. Males also sometimes exhibit these spots.

**Distribution**: Thick-lipped gourami, according to Day, range from the Irawadi River region of Rangoon (Burma) northward to Mandalay. Regan reports them in Tenasserim and Shan, the latter being somewhat questionable since *Colisa* species normally do not occur at these altitudes (mountains).

First introduced in 1904 (just one specimen) by Stueve (Hamburg). Scholze and Ploetzschke (Berlin) imported several in 1911.

**Maintenance**: Unpretentious and hardy fish for a well-planted community tank. Even the spawning season is relatively peaceful.

No particular water or food

*Colisa labiosa* female swimming to the male under their nest. Photo by the author.

needs, but can occasionally become somewhat shy.

**Breeding**: Spawn often in community tanks. At the appropriate time, separate the sexes a few days and nourish with mosquito larvae.

Introduce as a pair in thickly planted 20-gallon tank. Provide refuge for the female! As with *C. fasciata*, no plant parts are actively used in nestbuilding, but are used as base for the bubbles. The often irregularly shaped nest is flat and consists usually only of a little bubble-froth.

During each spawning act, about 10 to 100 clear eggs are released, which immediately rise up under the nest. During each spawning phase, about 400 to 600 eggs are produced. The young hatch in 24 hours and are free-swimming in another two days. At first they eat only infusoria, and then, in about another week, freshly hatched brine shrimp.

**Breeding strain**: In 1985 the yellow-to-orange gold *labiosa* appeared.

**Comments**: Occasionally, interesting behavior can be observed – spitting down prey. In conflict situations, an aggressive *C. labiosa* assumes a headstand with spread fins, and its mouth almost touching the bottom. The precise reason for this behavior or its biological purpose is unknown.

## *Colisa lalia* (Hamilton-Buchanan, 1822)

DWARF GOURAMI.

**Systematics**: First described in *Fishes of the Ganges*, pp. 120 and 372, as *Trichopodus lalius*. Invalid designations are *Trichogaster unicolor*, *Colisa unicolor*, and *cotra*.

*Colisa lalia* (HAMILTON–BUCHANAN, 1822)

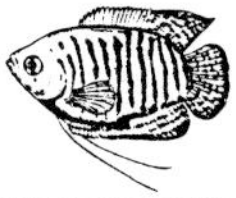

| | | | | | |
|---|---|---|---|---|---|
| 6/5 cm | 26/28° C | I | H1 | Z1 | A 1 |

| | | |
|---|---|---|
| D XV-XVII/7-10 | A XVII-XVIII/13-17 | mLR 27-28 |

**lalia** is from the native name in Assam for these fish, *Lal kholisha.*

**Description**: Sexual differentiation: The smaller females are usually fuller in the belly. Males are characterized during courtship and spawning, as well as at other times, by their more intensive coloration. Thickly-set lively fish which enthrall the aquarist, above all by the gala coloration of the male. The bold red body is striped with 10 to 14 diagonal, glistening turquoise blue bands. The unpaired fins are patterned to match. Even at first glance, the ocher-colored female harmonizes with it. During spawning, the coloration intensifies, turning brilliant blue.

**Distribution**: The dwarf gourami or threadfin are among the most common fish in the great river plains of northern India. They are at home in Pakistan (Punjab, Sind) as well as in the Ganges - Brahmaputra system (including Bangladesh). Reports of their presence in Borneo most certainly are due to an error. When the summer monsoon starts, the dwarf gourami leave the river system and move into the flooded flatland, whose shallow water zones now begin to warm up quickly. The ecological information given for *Colisa sota* also apply equally to *C. lalia.*

Dwarf gourami are economically useful fish in large areas of India. They usually appear as dried fish or as fishmeal in the local markets.

Fish introduced in 1875 in Paris as *C. unicolor*, and in 1903 by H. Stueve, Hamburg.

**Maintenance**: Ideal for well-planted community tank if the inhabitants are not too lively. At spawning time, however, the males can become aggressive, although they defend only the area around their nest.

Not fussy as far as water values or diet. Don't keep too cold! Occasionally timid.

The natural form of the Dwarf Gourami, *Colisa lalia*. This is a beautiful male. Photo by B. Kahl.

**Breeding**: Often spawn in community tank. Then the bubblenest and spawn can be transferred to a separate breeding tank.

For scientifically organized breeding, introduce by pairs in a small or moderately large tank planted with floating plants (*Riccia*, *Ceratopteris thalictroides*). For nest-building material, add Java moss or peat fibers. Plant the bottom well. Provide hiding spots for the female.

The male builds a compact nest of plant parts and frothy bubbles with a diameter of 2 to 2.4 inches. Mating occurs in the afternoon or in the evening.

A spawning phase produces about 300 to 700 eggs and takes two to three hours. Remove the female after spawning! The male is a careful guardian of the brood. The young hatch after about 24 hours, and leave the nest after a further two days. Now even the father should be removed. The first week they need small rotifers and tiny infusoria. Then they take freshly hatched *Artemia* nauplii.

**Strains**: The strains don't differ in behavior, maintenance or breeding from the wild form. Further breeding requires selection, since the offspring are not always genetically pure. Four strains or "breeds" are known:

*BLUE DWARF GOURAMI*

A strain, seen rather rarely, in which the blue in the male predominates over red parts. Even the back shimmers blue, and blue appears intensified also in the females. This is deceptive because the blue coloration is due to iridescence and is therefore greatly influenced by the direction of light incidence.

First introduced in 1979.

*NEON DWARF GOURAMI*

The males of this strain are similar in their color distribution to the wild form, but the blues are brighter.

First introduced in 1980.

The original first strain of *Colisa lalia*. This was the Red Dwarf Gourami, also called the Sunset and other such trade names. It was produced by Tan Guk Eng in Singapore in 1978. Photo by Yeok Ong who first distributed the fish in America in 1978.

Blue Dwarf Gourami, a tank-raised variety of *Colisa lalia.* Photo by the author.

*RAINBOW DWARF GOURAMI*

The males are uniformly orange red on the greater part of the body and caudal fin. Head and breast, as well as the forward parts of the dorsal and anal fins, are brilliant blue. The back shimmers greenish, often as if it were strewn with gold dust. Iris is orange-red. Females are without markings, aside from a dark spot at the root of the tail, but often shine somewhat bluish. In my opinion, one of the most beautiful *Colisa* strains.

First introduced in 1981.

*RED DWARF GOURAMI*

Similar to the rainbow dwarf gourami, but doesn't have blue in the head and throat areas where it's light yellowish gray. Dorsal fins of the male largely blue. There are strains with more orange and bright red.

The females can be like the wild form, or be without stripes.

First introduction in the fall of 1978 by the Singapore breeder and exporter Tan Guk Eng.

**Comments**: Dwarf gouramis occasionally spit well-aimed water drops at bits of food or prey located in the air above the water; the target is swamped and washed down into the water. Dwarf gouramis also spit now and then while building nests. Spawning males often make audible sounds when attacking intruders. In appearance and behavior, certainly one of the most recommendable labyrinth fish. Unfortunately, short-lived. Oldest age about two years.

## *Colisa sota* (Hamilton-Buchanan, 1822)

HONEY GOURAMI.

**Systematics**: First described in "An account of the fishes found in the River Ganges and its branches." Edinburg and London.

*Colisa sota* (HAMILTON–BUCHANAN, 1822)

| | | | | | |
|---|---|---|---|---|---|
| 4/4,5 cm | 25/28° C | I/II | H2 | Z2 | A 1 |
| D XVII-XIX/6-9 | | A XVII-XXII/11-15 | | | mLR 27-29 |

The magnificent Honey Gourami. The male is the more colorful of the pair, of course. These *Colisa sota* are in spawning condition. Photo by Burkhard Kahl.

p. 120/121. The author describes the females as *C. chuna* and the males as *C. sota*. Menon (1974) was the first (?) revisor to consider *C. chuna* a synonym.

A rather large number of differing characteristics (more spines in dorsal and anal fins, different patterning, differing markings on the young) call for a special position within the otherwise uniform genus.

**sota** is from a native name for the species.

**Description**: Sexual differentiation: Male in color has blue-black throat and abdomen. Anterior part of anal fin black. Body uniformly reddish brown. Spinous part of dorsal fin yellow. Female plain mustard, often with a dark longitudinal stripe from eye to root of tail. The males show this coloration, too, at other than spawning time, making it hard to tell them apart. Females are usually fuller in the abdomen, and, in contrast with the other threadfins or gouramis, *C. sota* females are larger than the males.

The honey gourami differs from the other *Colisa* species because it lacks transverse stripes.

**Distribution**: Brahmaputra lowlands from Dibrugarh in Upper Assam to Hooghly, not far to the west of Calcutta. Gathers more often than other *Colisa* species in large schools when not spawning. Spawning season in Assam usually occurs from April to October.

Optimal water temperature, according to field observations, is about 77° to 78.8°F. The usually slightly turbid water is very soft (1.4-2.8 DH), but has pH values of 6.8 to 8.5.

The fish established their bubblenests mostly in vegetation-rich shallow water, although you can find their nests in deeper water between floating plants, preferably between *Eichhornia crassipes* (water hyacinth), which also offers shelter to the adult fish. They also like to get into the flooded meadows (Krause, 1976). There, they anchor their nests between grass blades in almost standing water at a water level of 4 to 8 inches. Water temperature ranges between 80.6° and 86°F.

**Maintenance**: Honey gouramis like thickly planted tanks

(Above): *Colisa sota* male in its normal dress. (Right): A pair of *Colisa sota* spawning. Photos by the author.

with a few plant-free areas to allow swimming in the open. Floating plants! Well suited for the community tank if the inhabitants are quiet and friendly. Then they even spawn right away. Honey gourami are particularly suited to keeping in mini-tanks.

No problems as far as water requirements and diet are concerned, but don't keep too cold.

**Breeding**: Introduction by pairs is most advantageous in not too bright tanks of 10 gallons and up, landscaped with floating plants (Sumatra fern). Feed breeders separately with live food. The males build huge, flat bubblenests (diameter up to 15.8 inches), but

let them fall into disrepair after spawning.

The male gathers the eggs and carries them to a spawn raft or clump about as large as a cherry pit. The father constantly guards the eggs, which his salivary secretion sticks together. The spawn raft is easier to hide and defend from smaller fish than is a large bubblenest.

The 1/25″ crystal clear eggs at first float under the bubblenest and are not easily seen, not even for the father collecting them. Many honey gourami males place themselves at the edge of the bubblenest, and from there fire a rapid burst of waterdrops 1 to 1 1/2 inches into the air. When these drops fall back into the foam, they agitate the eggs an inch or so down so the father can recognize and gather them up easier.

In a few hours the eggs become yellow then finally grayish black. After 24 hours (at 86°F) to 35 hours (at 73.4°F) the now black-looking young hatch. In a day they are free-swimming and need food, which at first is infusoria.

In about a week they eat freshly hatched *Artemia*.

In good light, the head and flanks of the young shine a splendid blue in the first weeks. Rearing is somewhat easier than with other threadfins because the young are hardy and grow really fast.

## Genus *Ctenops* McClelland, 1845

**Number of Species**: 1

**Subfamily**: Macropodinae

**Systematics**: Possibly closely related to the genus *Trichopsis*, which in the past was included in the genus *Ctenops*. This assumption is, however, not definitely proven and for that reason is uncertain. So it's too soon to remove *Trichopsis* and its related genera along with the genus *Ctenops* from the subfamily Macropodinae, and to join them in a new subfamily, the "Ctenopinae."

**Ctenops** from ktenos (Greek) for comb; *ops* (Greek) for eye or countenance. The name refers to the serration of the anterior part of the orbit.

**Distribution**: Brahmaputra lowland south of the Himalaya chain up into the hill country.

## *Ctenops nobilis* McClelland, 1845

SHARP-HEADED GOURAMI.

**Systematics**: First described in *Calcutta Jour. Nat. Hist.* 5, p. 281 (1845, not 1844!)

**Synonym**: *Osphromenus nobilis* day.

**nobilis:** (Latin): known, famed, noble.

**Description**: Long, pointed snout, large mouth. Dorsal fin is set way back. Caudal fin rounded off. Sexes difficult to differentiate.

*Ctenops nobilis* McCLELLAND, 1845

| D IV-VII/6-8 | A III-IV/23-28 | mLR 28-34. | 10 cm |
|---|---|---|---|

The Sharp-headed Gourami, *Ctenops nobilis*, photographed by Horst Linke

Adult males are supposed to have a greatly lengthened first soft ray in the ventral fin. Brownish ground color. A silvery white, usually interrupted band starts at the posterior margin of the eye and ends at the lower part of the base of the caudal fin. In the upper part of the root of the tail there is occasionally a black eyespot rimmed with a bright halo.

**Distribution**: In the rivers of northeast Bengal, Assam, Bihar Sikkim and Bangladesh from the lowland into the hilly country.

First introduced in 1912 by Kropac, Hamburg.

**Maintenance and Breeding**: No details as to keeping or breeding because it is only rarely imported and is apparently rather susceptible to disease. Its origin in flowing water suggests need for adequate oxygen. Males are mouthbrooders.

## Genus *Malpulutta* Deraniyagala, 1937

**Number of Species**: 1

**Subfamily**: Macropodinae

**Systematics**: Build and reproductive behavior indicate that this genus is particularly close to the Southeast Asian genus *Parosphromenus*.

**Malpulutta** is from the Sinhalese *mal* (flower); *pulutta (Belontia signata)*, meaning "flower Belontia."

**Distribution**: Sri Lanka.

## *Malpulutta kretseri* Deraniyagala, 1937

MALPULUTTA.

**Systematics**: First described in *Malpulutta kretseri* – a new genus and species of fish from Ceylon, in *Ceylon Journ. Sci*, 351-353.

The species was divided by

*Malpulutta kretseri* DERANIYAGALA, 1937

| | | | | | |
|---|---|---|---|---|---|
| 9/4,5 cm | 25/27° C | II | H2 | Z1/2 | A 3 |
| D VIII-X/6 | | A XVI-XVII/9-11 | | | mLR 29-30 |

Deraniyagala into two subspecies: besides the nominate form, which is predominantly reddish brown in both sexes (found in Akurassa, Migahatauna, etc.), there is a somewhat smaller subspecies, that was described in 1958, *M. kretseri minor* (found in Kuruvita, Sabaragamuva Province), which has more blue in both sexes.

**kretseri:** from the discoverer of the fish, the Ceylonese lawyer De Kretser.

**Description**: Sexual differentiation: Adult males can be recognized easily by their spear-like caudal fin prolongation. The thread can be as long as 1 ½ inches. The dorsal fin, too, can have a thread-like prolongation.

The females are smaller.

At this time only the brownish-red nominate form is known in any detail: Brownish red ground color of body and unpaired fins. Female often uniformly colored.

Male occasionally has many irregularly distributed spots on the flanks. His ventral fins are light blue, the other fins have light blue margins.

Both sexes often exhibit a dark band which runs from the tip of the snout through the eye to the base of the pectoral fin.

**Distribution**: Endemic in Sri Lanka. Ranges widely, but not frequent in every place, and very seclusive. Inhabits running streams and irrigation canals, as well as ponds and puddles near small rivers. Water values according to Geisler: Temperature 25.7° to 26.3°C (approx. 78° to 79°F), pH 6.17 to 6.51, DH 0.19 to 0.43. According to Linke: Temperature 27.5°C (about 81°F), pH 6.6, DH 4.

First introduced in 1965 by Rolf Geisler and Herbert Bader (a pair).

**Maintenance**: A peaceful and often very seclusive fish that only comes into its own when tank-mates are serene and peaceful. They often remain almost motionless for long periods in their hideouts. The water should not be too hard and should be slightly acidic (peat filtration)! Frequent partial water changes and varied pond food are important, then the species can be kept and bred well in somewhat hard water. Mild water movement (slow filtration or aeration) is advantageous. Dry food is taken only after long hesitation. Good jumpers, so keep tank covered!

**Breeding**: Fish are best introduced as pairs. If need be, they will build bubblenests at the surface, but they prefer to build them in hollows ("caves") near the bottom. Pottery pots broken in half are accepted happily as artificial caves. At the appropriate water values and with varied diet of live food, the breeding and rearing of the young are quite easy.

**Interesting pair behavior**: Embracing occurs under the bubblenest. The male hugs the female by arching around her. After separating, the male remains motionless for about 15 seconds in a trance-like state. The whitish eggs are heavier than water, and after spawning is over they remain in the hollow formed by the male's body. In many cases, however, they slip slowly over the male's caudal fin and drop downwards, because the fish now stretch out a

bit. In that case, the female has sufficient time to gather the eggs from the body of the male. Then she puts them in the bubblenest. After every spawning act, the male swims to the nest and beds the eggs down once again.

Spawning lasts about 1 ½ hours. During the whole time the female can remain in the nest undisturbed, but will be chased out afterwards. The small number of eggs and their size indicate a particularly intensive brooding. The young hatch only after 45 hours (at 78.8°F) and are free-swimming on the sixth day after hatching. They immediately eat freshly hatched *Artemia* nauplii.

Natural breeding is preferable to artificial. In artificial breeding, an antifungal agent is needed to prevent fungal infection of the eggs, and aeration helps too.

This is a male Malpulutta. It is not in breeding condition or breeding dress. This *Malpulutta kretseri* is a very interesting breeder. The female actually collects the eggs and puts them into the bubblenest. Photo by the author.

*Parasphaerichthys ocellatus* PRASHAD und MUKERJI, 1929

D IV/4-6 A XIII/10-12 mLR 25+3

# Genus *Parasphaerichthys* Prashad and Mukerji, 1929

**Number of species**: 1

**Subfamily**: Macropodinae

**Systematics**: Closely related to the Southeast Asian genus *Sphaerichthys*, but distinguished from it by different jaws, absence of lateral line and distinctly broader body.

**Parasphaerichthys**: false *Sphaerichthys*, half a chocolate gourami.

**Distribution**: Northern Burma.

## *Parasphaerichthys ocellatus* Prashad and Mukerji, 1929

BURMESE CHOCOLATE GOURAMI.

**Systematics**: First described in "Fish of Indawgyi Lake," in *Rec. Ind. Mus.* 31, 216 ff.

**ocellatus** (Latin): with eye spot. Refers to the two dark, brightly bordered spots on the body, which are, however, characteristics of the young only.

**Description**: Sexual differences not known.

First described from two 23-mm (0.9-inch) young fish. The appearance of adults has not yet been described. I received a specimen of this species from Dr. Foersch which grew to a total length of 32 mm (1.3 inch).

The Burmese Chocolate Gourami, *Sphaerichthys ocellatus*. Photo by Dr. Walter Foersch.

Body ground color reddish brown with dark brown mottling. Body form similar to that of *Sphaerichthys acrostoma*, but differs in the rounded-off caudal fin, position of the ventral fins (which are attached behind the pectorals) and the width. The striking body width is especially apparent when seen from above.

According to the species description, both of the eyespots for which the fish is named are supposed to be characteristic. These can be seen in adults only when they are specifically looked for. Apparently the eyespots are characteristic only for young fish. They are dark, brightly rimmed spots, one about in the middle of the body under the end of the dorsal fin, the other at the root of the caudal fin.

**Distribution**: Small murky streams along the Kamaing Jade Road in the Myitkynia district near the greatest Burmese lake, the Indawgyi.

First introduced in the spring of 1978 by A. Werner, Munich.

**Maintenance**: Serene fish which usually remain motionless among the plants. Live foods.

## Genus *Pseudosphromenus* Bleeker, 1879

**Number of species**: 2

**Subfamily**: Macropodinae

**Systematics**: Differs from the genus *Macropodus* (or its synonym *Polyacanthus*) by differences in bony structure (Liem, 1963) and a different behavior (Vierke, 1975) as well as different distribution. *Pseudosphromenus* have sinking eggs and characteristic hanging larvae.

*Pseudosphromenus cupanus*, the Spike-tail Paradise Fish (female below). Photo by the author.

***Pseudosphromenus:*** false *Osphromenus*.

Osphro*menus* is synonymous with Osphro*nemus*, the edible gourami.

**Distribution**: Southern tip of India and Sri Lanka.

## *Pseudosphromenus cupanus* (Cuvier and Valenciennes, 1831)

SPIKE-TAILED PARADISE FISH.

**Systematics**: *Histoire naturelle des poissons* 7, p. 357; as *Polyacanthus cupanus*.

The species, long assigned to the genus *Polyacanthus* or *Macropodus*, was placed back in the genus *Pseudosphromenus* (established in 1879) in 1975. The

*Pseudosphromenus cupanus (CUVIER und VALENCIENNES, 1831)*

| | | | | | |
|---|---|---|---|---|---|
| 7/7 cm | 25/26° C | I/II | H1 | Z1 | A 2 |
| D XIII-XVII/5-7 | | A XVII-XX/9-13 | | | mLR 29-32 |

names *Polyacanthus cupanus* and *Macropodus cupanus* are thus synonyms. *cupanus* is supposed to refer to a river name on the Coromandel coast south of Madras.

**Description**: Sexual differentiation: When not spawning, mature females are identifiable only by their ovaries (by the method described for *Trichopsis pumilus*). The fish have to be looked at separately, in a bottle or tube, against a bright light source.

Males ready to spawn have intense reds in parts of the caudal, ventral and anal fins. Females are dark, often deeply black and often have a metallic sheen.

When not spawning, unpretentiously colored brownish. The young fish have a black spot at the base of the caudal fin. Long dorsal and anal fins. Caudal fins round in young, pointed in older fish. Fish imported from Goa often show a dark longitudinal stripe along the body, and also frequently show a dark spot behind the pectorals.

**Distribution**: Native to the coastal areas of southern India (Malabar and Coromandel coast) and Sri Lanka. All reports from Indo-China, Thailand, Burma and Malaya are extremely dubious. They probably are due to mistakes.

The fish are not rare, but are often overlooked because of their seclusive habits. They live in ditches, small bodies of water on the lowlands, and even occasionally get into the brackish tidal waters of the coast.

First introduced in 1903 by H. Stueve, Hamburg.

**Maintenance**: Despite its often unassuming appearance, a very recommendable aquarium fish because it is extremely content, peaceful and has such interesting mating behavior.

No particular water or dietary needs.

In communities with tank-mates which are too large or active, however, the black spike-tailed paradise fish are often timid. They tend to remain motionless for long periods in their hideouts.

**Breeding**: An especially easy-to-breed fish when they are first treated to living foods. It's best to introduce breeding fish by pairs into a landscaped 7 1/2-gallon tank provided with floating plants. A halved flower pot or a cemented stone cave serves as a brooding hollow. Black spike-tailed paradisefish build their nests directly at the surface, if necessary.

Interesting courtship is shown in which the male quickly embraces his now deeply black female, who lowers her head and does a real headstand. Even females that are not ready to spawn are usually not chased or injured by the male, as occurs with so many other labyrinth fish. A female ready to spawn can stay in the vicinity of the nest during the whole spawning phase. An embrace lasts 15 to 20 seconds and produces 5 to 30 white eggs which drop down separately to the bottom. Both parents gather them up and bring them to the nest. Many females are more active than the males in doing this.

Rearing the young offers little

*Pseudosphromenus dayi* spawning. They lay heavier-than-water eggs. The eggs are usually laid secretly in a cave. Photo by the author.

*Pseudosphromenus dayi* (STANSCH, 1913?)

| | | | | | |
|---|---|---|---|---|---|
| 7,5/6,5 cm | 25/26° C | I/II | H1 | Z1 | A 2 |
| D XIII-XVII/5-7 | | A XVI-XXI/10-12 | | | mLR 27-30 |

difficulty. The mothers, too, often participate in caring for the brood. If the male is removed, the female takes over care of the eggs or fry. Normally the parents don't often chase their free-swimming young.

## *Pseudosphromenus dayi* (Stansch, 1913?)

DAY'S PARADISE FISH.

**Systematics:** A valid first description by Koehler (1909) is lacking. The first (?) valid description is by K. Stansch (1913): "The labyrinth fish," Braunschweig, pp. 12–14.

The species had been considered since its mention by Day as a rose-colored variety of *Polyacanthus cupanus*, and as a subspecies of *Pseudosphromenus cupanus* or *Macropodus cupanus* since the observations of Koehler. This cannot be kept as it is. *P. dayi* is a valid species that in captivity is very difficult to hybridize with *P. cupanus*, which is explained by its completely different courtship behavior.

**Synonyms:** *Polyacanthus cupanus* var. *dayi*, *Macropodus cupanus dayi*, *Pseudosphromenus cupanus dayi*.

For a long time it was confused with *Parosphromenus deissneri*.

**dayi:** in honor of Francis Day (1829-1889).

**Description**: Adult males stand out because of their clearly longer drawn out dorsal and anal fin ends. The prolonged middle rays of the caudal fin (in both sexes) are longer in males. Females heavy with eggs show a characteristic irregularly brightened flank area.

Two dark converging stripes begin at the rear margin of the eye and end at the root of the caudal fin. These stripes are not always distinct. Body ground color is light tan to pinkish. Unpaired fins are reddish brown and brilliant light blue. Ventrals are occasionally deep red and likewise have a lengthened light blue soft ray.

**Distribution**: Almost every country in South and Southeast Asia is reported in the literature as the land of origin. All Southeast Asian reports are, however, more than questionable. The species doubtlessly comes from the south of India (Malabar coast), just as Day reports in 1889. The precise description by him of the species, then considered a variety, definitely precludes any confusion. First imported in 1907 by the Berlin firm Scholze and Poetzschke from Cochin from the Malabar coast.

**Maintenance**: Not fussy about water or diet. Peaceful and unobtrusive because of its often secluded lifestyle. So it's not so good for larger tanks. Most suitable for community living with small, peaceful fishes in well planted mini-tanks. *P. dayi* and *Colisa sota* are a good combination.

**Breeding**: Introduce as pairs in tanks landscaped with plants and artificial caves. Since the fish are peaceful together, a 5-gallon tank suffices. Preparatory feeding with live foods is good for spawning.

The bubblenest can be established under the cover of a rock or root cave, under horizontally growing *Cryptocoryne* leaves or directly at the surface of the water (under floating plant leaves).

Pursued females pacify their males by a characteristic raising of the head (*cupanus* lowers the head!) and by alternating jerks with the ventral fins.

Each of the 200 to 300 milk-white eggs measure exactly 1/25", including the "shell" or outer membrane. Both sexes often gather the eggs together. After spawning, the male alone takes over the care of the brood.

The young hatch in about 1½ days and are then 0.9 inch long. At first, they hang vertically, with the tail downwards, from the bubbles of the nest, or near them from floating plants. As soon as a few days after swimming free, the young eat *Artemia* nauplii. The parents don't usually pursue their young. Under favorable conditions, the young can be bred in three months.

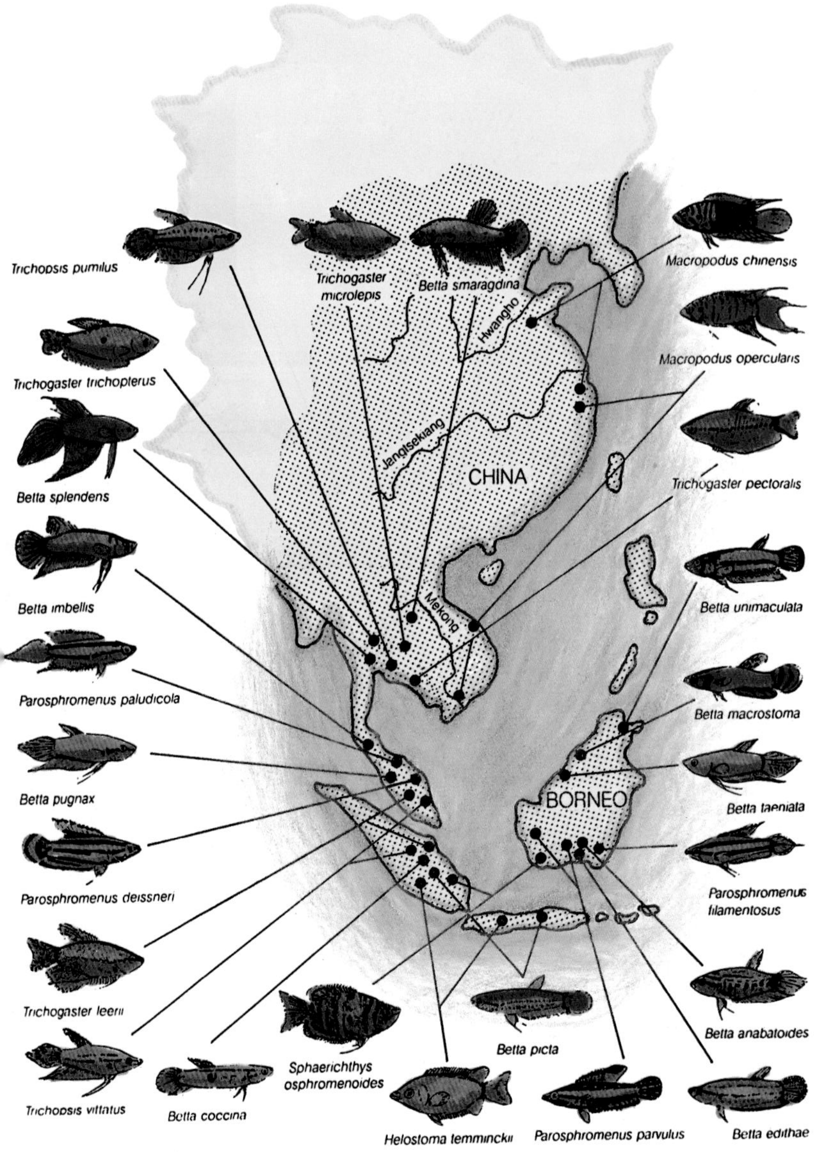


The distribution of labyrinth fishes in Southeast Asia. Note that there are no *Colisa* in this area! Drawn by J. Dittmar from a sketch by the author.

## LABYRINTH FISHES OF SOUTHEAST ASIA AND THE FAR EAST

The large rice plains of Thailand and China, the zoologically still unexplored jungles of the Malayan Peninsula, Sumatra and Borneo – that is all the heartland of labyrinth fishes. Here there are 10 genera and about 40 described species, and there are certainly still a large number of species as yet unknown to science.

The labyrinth fishes figure more importantly here in the native diet than they do even in Africa and India. Cast-nets and bottom nets, hooks and weirs, and many other devices are used to catch fish. Edible gouramis and kissing gouramis are farmed in ponds. The *Trichogaster* threadfins, too, in the Far East, and the *Anabas* climbing fish in Southeast Asia, are in demand as food fish.

Ornamental fish, too, in the broad sense are an old tradition in Southeast Asia and the Far East. Think of the goldfish of the Chinese and the Siamese fighting fish of the Thai. Today, Siamese fighting fish (*Betta splendens*) are still bred for fighting, and contests are still regular events. Large sums of money are often bet upon probable winners. These fights are, moreover, comparatively harmless, for only in exceptional cases are they fatal for the loser. That's completely the opposite to bullfights and cock fights.

Our oldest ornamentals for aquariums – the paradisefish – come from this area. The first paradisefish to go to Europe came from the east Chinese port city of Ningpo in 1869. Of the 20 surviving fish of the original 100, the Paris Museum employee Pierre Carbonnier received 12 males and five females. Two years later the quickly renowned fish breeder was able to market 600 paradisefish pairs.

Meanwhile, the capture of ornamental fish and the export of tropical aquarium fishes has become an important industry for some Southeast Asian and Far Eastern countries. In Hong Kong, Taiwan, Bangkok, and Singapore are many successful breeders and exporters for whom fighting fish and threadfins or gouramis (also in various cultivated varieties) still play a significant role.

## Genus *Anabas* Cuvier, 1816

CLIMBING PERCH.

**Number of species**: 2, including a species in Southeast Asia and the Far East.

**Comments**: The genus *Anabas* was discussed in detail in the section on the labyrinth fishes of India. In Indo-China, only *Anabas testudineus* is native. Details are given in an earlier section.

## Genus *Belontia* Myers, 1923

### *Belontia hasselti* (Cuvier, 1831)

JAVA COMBTAIL.

**Systematics**: First described

*Belontia hasselti* (CUVIER, 1831)

| | | | | | |
|---|---|---|---|---|---|
| 19,5/18 cm | 25/28° C | I | H1 | Z2 | A 3 |

| | | |
|---|---|---|
| D XVI-XX/10-13 | A XV-XVII/11-13 | mLR 30-32 |

in *Histoire naturelle des Poissons* 7 as *Polyacanthus hasselti.* Further synonyms: *Polyacanthus einthovenii, P. helfrichi, P. kuhli,* and *P. olivaceous.*

**hasselti:** from the name van Hasselt.

**Description**: Sexual differences are not clear, but the females are usually more stocky than the males, show less expressions of the comb, and have less pronounced finnage.

Oval body shape, grayish-brown ground color, every scale with dark margin. Comb-like pattern on caudal fin and soft rays of the dorsal and anal fins can be weaker or even absent, depending upon age, mood and origin. Young have eye-sized black spot in posterior portion of dorsal fin.

**Distribution**: Lakes and clear, slowly flowing waters of Malay Peninsula, Sumatra, Borneo and western Java.

First introduced by Dr. Axelrod in New York, 1952, as an incidental fish in a shipment from Singapore.

**Maintenance**: No special water or dietary needs. Relatively peaceful toward its own kind and other, not too small fishes. Completely safe with plants. Loves hideaways, but rarely uses them.

**Breeding**: Not difficult when diet consists of coarse live foods. Introduce as pairs in well planted tranquil tanks (25 gallons are enough). Water values are of no consequence for breeding.

The Java Combtail, *Belontia hasselti.* Photo by the author.

The male builds a nest of only a few bubbles, and often there is no nest at all. The eggs float at the surface and will be guarded by the male, who will also watch over the young which hatch in about two days. First food: freshly hatched *Artemia* nauplii.

**Comments**: Acclimated combtails often exhibit a peculiar resting behavior. They lay flat on their side on the bottom or lean up against rocks or plants, even during the day. They then take on a brown pattern easily confused with a leaf (mimicry). This sleep phase, lasting for several weeks, is interrupted about every 15 minutes to change the air in the labyrinth, for which they go briefly up to the water's surface, then return to their resting place.

## Genus *Betta* Bleeker, 1850

FIGHTING FISHES.

**Number of species**: Up to now, aside from the invalid duplicate descriptions, about 20 species have been described. There is doubtlessly a larger number of other species not yet described scientifically.

**Subfamily**: Macropodinae.

**Systematics**: The genus *Betta* is a problem child for taxonomists as well as for aquarists. The designation of several species is uncertain. That's due to the large number of species in the genus and the great similarity of many species; it's also partially due to inadequate species' descriptions. Quite an important factor in the difficulty with this genus is the relatively young age of the species. There was apparently, in evolutionary terms, a recent split into a large number of species (adaptive radiation), which have not yet morphologically differentiated much in many cases.

Ethologically, we can distinguish between mouthbrooders and bubblenest-building species within the genus. Doubtlessly, the mouthbrooders developed from the nest builders, presumably as an adaptation to life in flowing waters, in which bubblenests cannot hold.

Whether or not this adaptation occurred once or several times during the course of evolution in this genus, was not yet investigated. Morphologically, mouthbrooders differ from nest-builders in having larger heads. In essence, we can say that fighting fish with a head length that goes less than 3 ½ times into the standard length belong to the mouthbrooders (Vierke, 1979). The pressure of natural selection logically favors this situation, so this characteristic is not automatically an indication of any common origin of the mouthbrooders.

The proposal, largely based upon these differences, to divide the genus into two independent genera (bubblenest-building *Betta* and mouthbrooding "*Pseudobetta*" Richter, 1981) is not very helpful at this stage of the investigation, and has been resolutely rejected by most specialists. I, too, consider this division too hasty, for the reproduction type of many species is not yet unequivocally clarified.

**Distribution**: In all of Indo-China and the Malay Archipelago, except Burma, China, the Celebes (Sulawesi) and the Philippines.

**Comments**: I'm presenting 17 species here with their synonyms. Besides these names, the following two names (of uncertain species affiliation) appear in the literature: *B. bleekeri* (Regan) and *B. patoti* (Weber and De Beaufort).

## *Betta akarensis* Regan, 1910

AKAR BETTA.

**Systematics**: First described in "The Asiatic fishes of the family *Anabantidae*," *Proc. Zool. Soc.* London, p. 779. The date of the first description is again erroneously reported as 1909, as

*Betta akarensis* REGAN, 1910

| | | |
|---|---|---|
| D 0/8 | A I/27 | mLR 31 |

are also *B. fusca*, *B. taeniata,* and other species published in this work. In fact, Regan's work was first published in April, 1910.

**akarensis:** from the Akar river, where it was discovered.

**Description**: The first scientific description was of only one 2 ½″ specimen–an elongated, brownish fish with dark fins and a dark longitudinal stripe through the head and crossing the eye.

The species should be distinguished from *B. patoti*, according to M. Weber and L. F. De Beaufort (1922), above all, by the dorsal fin base being clearly closer to the caudal fin than to the head. With *akarensis*, on the other hand, the dorsal fin should lie somewhat in the middle between both points.

in *Nat. Tijdschr. Ned. Indie* I, p. 269/270.

This species belongs to the mouthbrooding fighting fish group which also includes *B. pugnax*, from which it is distinguished by a rounder head profile, absence of iridescent scales on the head of the male, etc.

Regan (1910) as well as Weber and De Beaufort (1922) refer to fish from very different localities (e.g., Sumatra, Malay Peninsula) which many times include other species as well. The details given here (description, maintenance, breeding) refer only to the two types from Bleeker's original description and field specimens brought from a typical site (Bandjermasin).

**anabatoides**: similar to the

*Betta anabatoides* BLEEKER, 1850

| | | | | | |
|---|---|---|---|---|---|
| 12 cm | 26/28° C | I/II | H2 | Z3 | A 3 |

| | | |
|---|---|---|
| D 0-II/6-8 | A I-II/22-30 | mLR 28+3 — 32+2 |

**Distribution**: The species was described in association with the Akar River in Sarawak, Western Borneo. The species is no longer imported alive, thus there is no information on coloration of the living fish, or how to keep or breed it.

## *Betta anabatoides* Bleeker, 1850

GREAT BORNEO BETTA.

**Systematics**: First description

The Great Borneo Betta, *Betta anabatoides.* Photo by Dr. Walter Foersch.

*Betta balunga* HERRE, 1940

| D I/7 | A 28-29 | mLR 30-31 | 68 mm |
|---|---|---|---|

climbing fish *Anabas*.

**Description.** Sexual differentiation: Adult males have longer drawn-out dorsal and anal fin ends. Females are thicker during spawning.

Hardy, large-headed fish. Mouth relatively small. Lips end just before or at the forward edge of the eye.

Middle caudal fin rays are lengthened, dorsal and anal fins drawn out. Variable coloration. Ground color ochre often with irregular dark diagonal stripes or with two dark, parallel longitudinal stripes beginning at the forehead and ending at the rear edge of the eye.

**Distribution**: Typical site is Borneo near Bandjarmasin. Presumably in all of Borneo (except the northern part). Native waters usually quite acidic, cola-color with conductivity of 5-30 microsiemens and temperature of 80.6°-86°F. Usually in heavily vegetated bank zone of slowly flowing waters.

First introduction, March, 1978, by Mr. & Mrs. Foersch, Mrs. Korthaus and Mr. Hanrieder.

**Maintenance**: Keep in pairs. Ample live foods. This fish is a mouthbrooder that, according to the observations of Dr. Foersch, exhibit a spawning behavior corresponding to *B. pugnax*. Spawning coloration differs strikingly from that of *B. pugnax*. Upper third of body is dark gray-brown, the lower two-thirds bright, almost white, with two delicate dark longitudinal stripes in the posterior half (according to Foersch). Young hatch after about 80 hours (at 78.8°F). Eight days later they are released by the father and not guarded any longer.

## *Betta balunga* Herre, 1940

BALUNG BETTA.

**Systematics**: First described in "New species of fishes from the Malay Peninsula and Borneo," *Bull. Raffles Mus.* 16, p. 44.

**balunga:** from the Balung River in North Borneo.

**Description**: A dark longitudinal stripe present starting somewhat under and behind the root of the pectoral fins and continuing posteriorly over the center of the caudal fin. Coloration of the live fish is unknown.

**Distribution**: Balung River near the city of Tawan (North Borneo). The species does not appear to be numerous and has not been imported yet.

## *Betta bellica* Sauvage, 1884

SLENDER BETTA.

**Systematics**: First described in *Bull. Soc. Zool. de France* IX, p. 217.

Possibly identical with *B. fasciata*.

**bellica** (Latin): bellicose, war-like.

**Description**: Sexes hardly distinguishable by coloration. Fins

*Betta bellica* SAUVAGE, 1884

| | | | | | |
|---|---|---|---|---|---|
| 11/9 cm | 26/28° C | II | H2 | Z2 | A 3 |
| D I/10 | | A II/30-32 | | | mLR 35 |

of the male more pronounced, caudal fin pointed. Largest bubblenest-building fighting fish. Elongated. Relatively small-headed. Body brownish with light green rimmed scales. Vertical fins brownish-red with metallic green and golden orange shimmering membranes.

**Distribution**: In the south of the Malay Peninsula. Lives exclusively in vegetation-rich, quiet water. In 1984 I captured several specimens in a street ditch near Ayer Hitam. Water 82.4°F., 33 microsiemens, pH 4.6. Other, incidental fish: *Betta imbellis* (many), *Anabas testudineus*, dwarf *Rasbora*, *Puntius pentazona*.

First introduced into Germany in 1913.

The Slender Betta, *Betta bellica*. Photo by the author.

**Maintenance**: Relatively aggressive toward their own species, so keep only in pairs. A community tank with several *Betta imbellis* went smoothly. Not fussy as concerns water or food. Likes to eat mosquito larvae, *Tubifex*, small rainworms. Loves thick vegetation here and there, but is not shy after getting used to the surroundings, and shows itself often.

**Breeding**: Bubblenest builder. Female ready to spawn exhibits several transverse bands. Spawning behavior is similar to that of other bubblenest-building fighting fish. After spawning, the eggs rain down, and are snapped up by the male. In *B. bellica*, the eggs – or at least the largest portion of the spawn – remain in a

| | | | | | |
|---|---|---|---|---|---|
| 14cm | 25/26 °C | I/II | H1 | Z3 | A3 |
| D 0/7-9 | | A II/25 | | | mLR 33+2 |

pocket which the female forms with her pectoral fins, and presses against her body. The male can take the spawn from this pocket. All this is a method to reduce the risk in transferring eggs.

Not very reliable in brood care. The young grow fast.

## *Betta climacura* Vierke, 1988

LADDERTAIL FIGHTING FISH

**Systematics**: "*Betta climacura* n. sp. from western Borneo and remarks on *Betta taeniata* Regan 1910." *Das Aquarium.* At first this species was confused with *B. anabatoides;* later it was incorrectly identified as *B. taeniata* and presented as such in aquarium journals.

**klimax** (Greek): = ladder; **oura** (Greek): = tail. After the crossbands between the caudal rays, which remind one of the rungs of a ladder.

**Description:** One of the largest *Betta* species; the males are distinguished by their lance-shaped, extended tail fin, whose fin rays are connected by runglike transverse markings. The typical blue markings in the head area are lacking.

**Distribution:** Sarawak, from Kuching to Brunei. Beneath roots and rocks along the banks of small, lowland rivers; also in residual pools. In Bako National Park, supposedly the only species of fish adapted to life in the occasionally extremely swift currents of rocky pools and rills.

**Maintenance:** Does not disturb plants, but is occasionally quarrelsome with its own kind. Not difficult to satisfy, takes dry food but prefers small worms. Likes to jump so cover tank well.

**Breeding:** Mouthbrooder. Reproductive behavior exactly like *B. pugnax*, except that the female, in contrast to *pugnax*, has pronounced body stripes.

These are NOT *B. taeniata* even though they are so named in most books. This is *B. climacura.* Photo by the author.

*Betta coccina* VIERKE, 1979

| | | | | | |
|---|---|---|---|---|---|
| 4,5/4 cm | 25/28° C | II | H2 | Z3 | A 3 |
| D 0-II/7-10 | | A III/19-27 | | | mLR 29-31+3 |

Male Wine-red Betta, *Betta coccina*. Photo by the author.

## *Betta coccina* Vierke, 1979

WINE-RED BETTA.

**Systematics**: First described as "*Betta coccina* nov. spec; a new fighting fish from Sumatra," in *Das Aquarium*, pp 288–289.

**coccinos**: wine red

**Description**: Males more colorful with longer drawn-out dorsal and anal fins. Body elongated, only slightly compressed, with rather round head profile. Older male juveniles and young males have intensely wine-red body and fins. Eyes iridescent green. Often an eye-sized iridescent green spot on the flank. Older fish lose the spot on the flank and become more brownish.

**Distribution**: Live very secluded in tangle of water plants or among foliage which has dropped down to the bottom of quiet waters. Originally described from Central Sumatra near Jambi. Now they can also be found on the Malay Peninsula. Barbara and Allan Brown (personal communication) describe a site near Rawang (18 ½ miles north of Kuala Lumpur): flat, foliage filled puddles (0-11.8 inches deep) in the shade of the forest, in very brownish, warm (about 80°F) water, pH 6, and hardness less than DH 6.

First introduced in 1977 by Dr. Liem, Djakarta.

**Maintenance**: Must have hiding places, preferably in thickly

planted tanks with their own species, and with many floating plants. Cover the tank carefully. Change water frequently. Susceptible to *Oodinium*.

**Breeding**: Introduce them in pairs into tanks with many floating plants. Bubblenest builders which cannot easily be made to spawn. Needs, besides higher temperature, probably soft water and hardy live foods. Young grow slowly, but soon show attractive red coloration.

**Comments**: In 1985 Schaller described the fish from the Malay Peninsula as *Betta tussyae*. According to his information they possess larger scales and a more broadly attached dorsal fin, although he himself writes that otherwise they strongly resemble *coccina*. Without more comparative details on morphometric and meristic values, it is difficult to decide upon the species status. I tend to consider this form as a subspecies of *coccina*, for the agreement goes much further than the first description indicates. For example, in the Malayan form there is also the brilliant green spot on the flank in many young males, which disappears again later (personal communication from Barbara and Allan Brown).

*Betta edithae.*
Photo by the author.

## *Betta edithae* Vierke, 1984

EDITH'S BETTA.

**Systematics**: "*Betta taeniata*" (Regan, 1910) and *Betta edithae* sp.n, two fighting fish from southern Borneo, "*Das Aquarium*" pp. 58-63.

A completely new form (same species?) found in southern Thailand and previously reported erroneously as *Betta taeniata*. *B. edithae*, too, was called *B. taeniata* or *B.* spec. affin. *taeniata* before the description.

**edithae:** from Edith Korthaus, who participated in the discovery of the species.

**Description**: Sexual differentiation: Female usually thicker-set, and exhibits bold

*Betta edithae* VIERKE, 1984

| | | | | | |
|---|---|---|---|---|---|
| 9,5/9 cm | 26/28° C | I/II | H2 | Z3 | A 3 |
| D I/6-8 | | A I-II/25-28 | | mLR 28+3 — 32+2 | |

*Betta fasciata*. This is a pair, with the male in the foreground. The female is hardly visible in this picture. Photo by Dave Roddy.

longitudinal stripes during courtship and spawning.

Small eyes. Short fins. Caudal fin round, but individual fin rays extend out beyond the edge. Three dark longitudinal stripes, the middle one passing through the eye, the lower one joining the middle one at the root of the tail. Stripes visible only sometimes. Body ground color beige, often blue glistening points on the scales. Anal fin of the male spotted with blue and darkly bordered. Dorsal fin and particularly caudal fin exhibits striking dark spots or stripes between the fin rays. Forehead line straight, but often indented in older fish.

**Distribution**: In all of southern Borneo relatively common, especially in slowly flowing waters. Possibly also on Malay Peninsula (southern Thailand).

First introduced in March, 1978, by Edith Korthaus, Dr. Walter Foersch and Alfred Hanrieder.

**Maintenance**: Quiet and tolerant pets in the tank, with no particular water or dietary needs. They like to eat small worms.

**Breeding**: Mouthbrooders. Introduce as pairs. Do not disturb. Female initiates spawning and defends the territory for a short time. Then she circles the male repeatedly until he embraces her. The spawning usually occurs on the bottom, where the male's body makes a U-shape. After spawning, the eggs are held in the pocket formed by the male's body or on his anal fins. As soon as the female is released from the embrace, she collects the eggs from the male's body. Then she gives him the eggs by placing herself diagonally in front of him and spitting them over to him. The young are released in about 10 days. Unfortunately, however, many broods perish after one to three days of mouthbrooding care.

## *Betta fasciata* Regan, 1910

BANDED BETTA.

**Systematics**: First described in "The Asiatic fishes of the family

*Betta fasciata* REGAN, 1910

| | | | | | |
|---|---|---|---|---|---|
| 10/8 cm | 26/28° C | II | H2 | Z2/3 | A 3 |
| D I/9-10 | | A II/30 | | | mLR 34-36 |

Anabantidae" in *Proc. Zool. Soc.* London, p. 782.

Presumably only a geographical form of *B. bellica.*

**fasciata** (Latin): striped or banded.

**Description**: Slender fish strongly resembling *B. bellica* in appearance, but are supposed to have a deeper tail base (*bellica* height of caudal peduncle at base of caudal fin goes 1.8 times into the head length, *fasciata* height goes 1.3 times). Importation of *fasciata* is necessary for certain differentiation from *bellica.* The dark transverse bands for which the species is named are scarcely visible in the living fish. Males shine splendidly in velvet blue during spawning periods.

**Distribution**: The species was originally collected by Mersen on the small island of Deli, about 9 miles south of the western tip of Sumatra. It is also found on Sumatra, and is supposed to inhabit the opaque, almost coffee-brown ponds and ditches there. Not common, so rarely imported. First imported in 1905 as *B. bellica* by J. Reichelt, of Conradshoehe.

**Maintenance and Breeding**: These fish need a large, well planted tank and should be kept in pairs. Bubblenest builders.

## *Betta foerschi* Vierke, 1979

FOERSCH'S BETTA.

**Systematics**: First description: "*Betta anabatoides* and *Betta foerschi* spec. nov., two fighting fish from Borneo," in *Das Aquarium*, pp. 386-388.

**foerschi:** from Dr. Walter Foersch, Munich, one of the discoverers of the species.

**Description.** Sexual differentiation: Male slenderer, with more drawn-out anal fin. Transverse bands on the gill covers are black in males and reddish-black in females. Courting males have orange-red gill cover bands, females golden ones.

Elongated fish with relatively small, broad head. Head profile rounded. Relatively short-finned, caudal fin rounded. Characteristic feature sometimes on the front part of the gill cover (preoperculum) and gill cover

*Betta foerschi* VIERKE, 1979

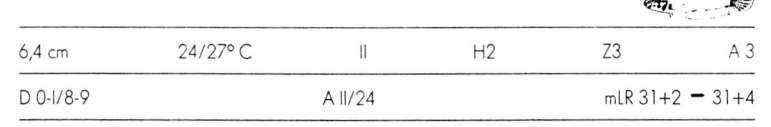

| | | | | | |
|---|---|---|---|---|---|
| 6,4 cm | 24/27° C | II | H2 | Z3 | A 3 |
| D 0-I/8-9 | | A II/24 | | | mLR 31+2 – 31+4 |

(operculum): a dark transverse band. Two transverse bands are occasionally superimposed with two dark longitudinal bands. Fright coloration: transverse body stripes. During courtship (and spawning), the bodies and vertical fins of both sexes can turn almost black.

**Distribution**: Southern Borneo. The only known site is the Mentaya River system about 150 miles northwest of Bandjarmasin. The fish were captured in the swampy bank zone of a small, rather rapidly flowing stream.

*Betta foerschi.* Photo by Dr. Walter Foersch after whom this fish was named. Dr. Foersch lives in Munich, Germany and is a very active labyrinth fish enthusiast. He is a physician.

*Betta fusca* REGAN, 1910

| | | | | | |
|---|---|---|---|---|---|
| 8,5/7,5 cm | 25/27° C | I/II | H2 | Z3 | A 3 |
| D 0/8-9 | | A II/21-24 | | | mLR 29-32 |

Water very dark, very acidic, conductivity 75 microsiemens, 75.2°F. Other fish present: *Rasbora kalochroma*, *Luciocephalus pulcher*, small snakeheads.

First imported in March, 1978, by Dr. Foersch, Edith Korthaus and Alfred Hanrieder.

**Maintenance and Breeding**: When young, relatively lively and big eaters (living foods if at all possible) then later somewhat quieter. Hide often in plants. If possible, keep separate from other fish. Breeding not yet successful. Probably mouthbrooders.

## *Betta fusca* Regan, 1910

BROWN BETTA.

**Systematics**: First description in "The Asiatic fishes of the family Anabantidae" in *Proc. Zool. Soc. London*, p. 780.

Belongs to the *pugnax* form group and can not be distinquished meristically, or only with very great difficulty, from the closely related *pugnax*.

**fusca** (Latin): dark, dusky, in reference to the dark coloration of the fins in the preserved (!) type specimens. The name used by the Germans, *brown fighting fish*, describes the actual appearance aptly.

**Description**: Adult males have longer, drawn-out anal fin ends and shining scales in the gill-cover region. Female fuller. Relatively slender, sharp-snouted fish of the *pugnax* type, that is, with lengthened middle caudal fin rays

The Peaceful Betta, *Betta imbellis.* Photo by the author.

and lengthened anal fin ends.

In states of contentment, body color and fins are uniformly reddish-brown. Iris shining green or red. Greenish sheen spots on scales.

**Distribution**: Sumatra. Dr. Etzel captured the species in a slowly flowing stream near Pajakumba (western Sumatra). The 8-12-inch wide and 4- to-12-inch deep stream was clear and the temperature was 77°F. Many rocks of various sizes in the water provided hiding spots for the fish.

First introduced in May, 1971, by Dr. V. Etzel.

**Maintenance**: Hardy. Don't keep too warm, and arrange for water circulation (rotating pump). Accepts all food, and likes small and medium sized rainworms.

**Breeding**: Mouthbrooders. Introduce in pairs for breeding. Behavior similar to that of *B. pugnax.*

## *Betta imbellis* Ladiges, 1975

PEACEFUL BETTA.

**Systematics**: First described in "*Betta imbellis* nov. spec, the friendly fighting fish" in *DATZ* 28, pp. 262-265.

*Betta imbellis* is closely related to *B. splendens.*

**imbellis** (Latin): unwarlike, peaceful.

**Description**: Male larger, more colorful and with more well defined finnage. Delicate *Betta* very similar in coloration to the wild *Betta splendens*, but clearly slimmer.

Body of male brownish or blue-gray, scales with dark margins. Black when in full color, scales with bluish shining spots. Peripheral portions of caudal fin, point of anal fin and middle portion of pelvic fins boldly red. Tips of pelvic fins white. Dark flecks on hind portion of dorsal fin.

Females ready to spawn are light, with several irregular dark transverse stripes on body. Fins often tinged reddish. There are several color varieties.

**Distribution**: On the whole .Malay Peninsula from the Kra

*Betta imbellis* LADIGES, 1975

| | | | | | |
|---|---|---|---|---|---|
| 5/4 cm | 26/28° C | I/II | H1 | Z1 | A 2 |
| D 0-I(-III)/(5-17-9 | | A (II-)III/22-25 | | | mLR 27-32 |

isthmus to the extreme south, in swampy areas, puddles and rice paddies. Water, as a rule, is soft, neutral to moderately acidic, and ranges in temperature from 77° to 95°F.

Ecologically very adaptive, but prefers vegetation-filled waters with little current. First introduced in 1970 by Schaller.

**Maintenance**: The name *imbellis* (peaceful) is misleading, because territorial males often battle rather furiously. In northwestern Malaysia, natives use them in fish-fighting contests, similar to the use made of *Betta splendens* in Thailand. A thickly planted tank with a surface of 32 × 12 inches, and including floating plants, can house about four males so that even over a longer period they won't unduly rip up their finnage, considering their small size and the correspondingly little space they require. Otherwise, for communities, use only peaceable small fish that are not too rough. No particular water or dietary needs.

**Breeding**: Introduce in pairs after preliminary feeding with

A male *Betta imbellis*. Photo by the author.

ample live food. Females ready for spawning exhibit a white genital papilla. Not very productive, producing only 130 to 160 eggs during each spawning phase. With a good diet, however, they spawn weekly.

Males are bubblenest builders. Embracing occurs as with *B. splendens*. The bean-shaped, milky-whitish eggs rain down from the genital opening of the female, who remains in a frozen trance-like state after spawning even when the male has long recovered from it. Then the male stations himself under the female and snaps up the individual eggs, which are dropping to the bottom. Then he beds them down in the froth of his bubblenest. During the spawning phase, the female often helps to gather up and bed down the spawn. The case of the brood care later, however, is taken over fully by the male alone. Egg diameter (without enclosing membrane) is 0.03 inch.

The young at first feed on infusoria, but soon also eat *Artemia* nauplii. Rearing is not difficult.

*Betta macrostoma* REGAN, 1910

| | | | | | |
|---|---|---|---|---|---|
| 14/10 cm | 24/26° C | II | H2 | Z3 | A 4 |
| D 11 | | A 26 | | | mLR 32 |

This beautiful male *Betta macrostoma* has been called the Brunei Beauty by Dr. Axelrod. He brought the first live specimens out of Brunei. This photograph shows a newly captured male. The fish was collected and photographed by Heiko Bleher. A closeup of the tail of this same fish, on top of the facing page, shows the rays protruding past the fin membrane.

## *Betta macrostoma* Regan, 1910

**Systematics**: First described in "The Asiatic fishes of the family Anabantidae," in *Proc. Zool. Soc.* London, p. 778.

**macrostoma** (Greek): with large mouth opening.

**Description:** Sexual differentiation: Male larger and more colorful. The large mouth opening is characteristic, and goes to just under the middle of the eye. Younger fish and females have two parallel dark stripes longitudinally along the body, ending at the root of the tail. A dark spot at the root of the tail lies between the ends of the two stripes.

Males in color have orange bodies and fins. Posterior portion of the dorsal fin usually shows an eye-sized black spot rimmed with orange. Two or three thick, dark transverse bands under the eye and at the margin of the gill cover. An attractive fish.

**Distribution**: Regan reported Sarawak as the discovery site. Recently Dr. Herbert Axelrod found them in Brunei near Kampong Labi (4° 25′ N, 114° 28′

A male *Betta macrostoma* dancing before a female. Photo by Dr. Herbert R. Axelrod.

A nice male *Betta macrostoma*, above. Can you see the *Betta macrostoma* hiding in the leaf in the lower photo? Photos by Dr. H.R. Axelrod.

E). There the species lives in the tranquil, dark corners of a large elevated lake, in the shade of fallen trees. The fish is not common there.

Water temperature is reported at 75°F, extremely soft and acidic. It prefers running waters at higher altitudes.

In April, 1984, *macrostoma* arrived in Europe, where it was soon bred (T. Schulz of Buedingen). In the USA, the first fish appeared as early as 1982 (Axelrod), but these two fish were of differing color pattern and died within 90 days of import.

**Maintenance**: It's best to keep them in larger tanks with plants to provide cover. Live foods if possible, especially worms. No special water needs. Susceptible to infections, but fish bred in captivity are not so susceptible.

**Breeding**: Males are mouthbrooders. The female gathers up the eggs after spawning and transfers them to the male. The eggs are, however, like with *B. pugnax* or *picta*, spit out to the male, but not directly mouth to mouth, according to Dr. Axelrod. Mouthbrooding care lasts 21 days. The 40 to 120 young fish go for freshly hatched *Artemia* immediately upon release from the mouth (according to Schulz, 1985). Dr. Axelrod claims that Schulz's fish is a different species.

## *Betta picta* (Cuvier & Valenciennes, 1846)

JAVAN BETTA.

**Systematics**: First described in *Hist. naturelle des poissons* 18, p. 385 as *Panchax pictum.*

*B. trifasciata* Bleeker, 1850 is a frequently used synonym, and *B. rubra* Perugia, 1893 is also a synonym for this species, even if Regan reports A. III. My own investigations at the Natural History Museum of Vienna indicated that "*trifasciata,*" too, can have three anal spines (Vierke, 1981c). Regan's illustration shows a *Betta picta* with fright markings.

Javan Betta, *Betta picta* male. Photo by the author.

*Betta picta* (CUVIER & VALENCIENNES, 1846)

| | | | | | |
|---|---|---|---|---|---|
| 5,5/4,5 cm | 25/28° C | I/II | H1 | Z1 | A 3 |
| D (0-)I(-II)/6-8 | | A (I-)II(-III)/18-21 | | mLR 27+2 – 29+1 | |

**picta** (Latin): painted, colorfully spotted.

**Description**: Male often blue-throated. Anal fins uniformly reddish-brown at the base, with shining blue spots and dark edging. Anal fins of the female unmarked (Java form) or with numerous brownish flecks (Sumatra form). Female deeper-set.

A small, short-finned mouthbrooder with rounded caudal fin. Males, especially, can have attractive brownish-red bodies and finnage at spawning time. Otherwise, there are three parallel longitudinal stripes, hence the old name *trifasciata* (three-striped).

**Distribution**: Java, Sumatra, Bangha and Biliton. Not uncommon in flowing waters and around lakes. Found at altitudes up to 5,200 feet, and tolerates temperatures there of about 60.8°F.

**Maintenance**: Peaceful and contented, and also suitable for community tanks. No special water or dietary requirements.

**Breeding**: In community tanks, too, you can occasionally see mouthbrooding males, but it's best to introduce the fish by pairs in smaller, well-planted tanks with an open area which will serve as a spawning ground. Easier to breed than the other mouthbrooding *Bettas*.

During spawning, the female dominates and defends the territory. Embracing is at the bottom, rarely at higher levels. After spawning, the eggs remain in the pocket formed by the male's body, from which the female takes them. Then she spits them over to the male until he accepts them. A female produces up to 125 eggs, but the male can not take the whole batch. He swallows a portion of it (he has a rounded belly after the spawning phase!) and so survives the mouthbrooding time of almost two weeks quite well. The female should be removed after spawning so that the male can remain undisturbed during the brooding. The young are released when they are about 0.03 inch (7-mm) long, and are not pursued by the father. The young feed immediately on *Artemia* nauplii.

## *Betta pugnax* (Cantor, 1850)

PENANG BETTA.

**Systematics**: First described in "Cat. Malayan Fishes," in *Journ. Asiat. Soc. Bengal.* Vol. 18, p. 1066 as *Macropodus pugnax*.

In Southeast Asia the *pugnax* group includes a whole group of closely related, mouthbrooding *Bettas* that all resemble one another. All are characterized by lengthened middle rays in the

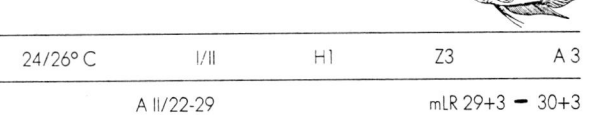

*Betta pugnax* (CANTOR, 1850)

| | | | | | |
|---|---|---|---|---|---|
| 10/9,5 cm | 24/26° C | I/II | H1 | Z3 | A 3 |
| D 0-II/7-9 | | A II/22-29 | | | mLR 29+3 – 30+3 |

*Betta pugnax* spawning. Both fish are retrieiving the eggs. Photo by the author.

caudal fin. The anal fin, when laid back, always reaches beyond the middle of the caudal fin. Also part of this group are *B. anabatoides* from Borneo, an anabantoid-similar form from the island of Sumba, which I saw at the Natural History Museum in Vienna (No. 7254-581), *B. fusca* from Sumatra and the actual *B. pugnax* from the mainland.

I also have available preserved specimens from central Thailand and Cambodia (Phnom Penh), which are also to be assigned to the *pugnax* group. They won't be given any further attention here, however, for they are possibly separate species, although they are closely related to *pugnax*.

The same applies to *B. macrophthalma* (Regan, 1910) and *B. brederi* (Meyers, 1935).

**pugnax** (Latin): bellicose, warlike.

**Description**: Males at spawning time more colorful than

*Betta pugnax*, a pair. Photo by the author.

females, with shining scales on the gill covers. Females compact, with less developed fins.

All body scales have greenish iridescent spots, particularly in specimens captured in the wild. Caudal fin spatulate or pointed. Body form is dependent upon water current (slimmer in flowing waters, but older fish in quiet tanks bullishly thickset).

**Distribution**: If peripheral groups are not considered, then range is limited to Malay Peninsula.

Lives in the flowing waters of forested hilly country. Requires either submerged plants or else vegetation from above the water which hangs down and dips into the water, or even foliage soaked down into the water. Water temperature seldom above 78.8°F, usually around 75.2°F. Soft water.

First imported in 1905 by J. Reichelt, of Conradshoehe.

First bred in 1912 by J. Hipler of Berlin.

**Maintenance**: Peaceful fish which are friendly toward their own as well as other species. Their Latin name *pugnax* is completely misleading! They need hiding spots and like moving water. Easy to keep as far as water and diet are concerned. Favorite food consists of small and moderately large worms.

**Breeding**: Keep in pairs in well planted, quiet tanks. Give ample live food, change water frequently. Water should not be too hard.

Mouthbrooders. Female initiates spawning by swimming around the male. They embrace on the bottom. After the eggs are laid, the male loosens his embrace, but still remains in a U-shape on the bottom. The female can now scoop up the eggs from his anal fin, like from a bowl. Then she stations herself diagonally in front of him and spits out the eggs at him. The young are free-swimming in about 10 days. These fish spawn freqently, though the parents usually eat the spawn after one to three days.

## *Betta smaragdina* Ladiges, 1972

EMERALD BETTA.

**Systematics**: First described in "*Betta smaragdina* nov. spec." in *DATZ*, pp. 190-191.

**smaragdina** (Latin): emerald.

**Description**: Males have larger fins, females lack red in pelvic fins. Elongated, with relatively small head, round caudal fin. Both sexes dark, almost black, when in color, with large green shining

*Betta smaragdina* LADIGES, 1972

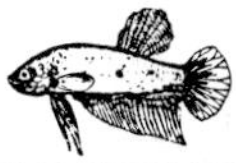

| | | | | | |
|---|---|---|---|---|---|
| 7/6 cm | 26/28° C | I/II | H1 | Z1 | A 3 |
| D I-II/7-9 | | A IV-V/22-26 | | | mLR 31-35 |

spots on every scale. In the resting phase, coloration is rather unassuming, with two dark stripes running longitudinally and parallel along the body.

**Distribution**: Northeast Thailand in overgrown, weedy ditches and ponds. D. Schaller found them first in the rice fields, in the muddy-water-filled footprints of the water buffalo. A typical locality is the village of Nongkhai on the Mekong near the Laotian capital of Vientiane, on the banks of the bordering river.

First introduced in 1970 by Schaller.

**Maintenance**: Tolerates other fishes, exhibits full coloration in the community tank, but only rarely. Can be kept well with small *Rasboras*, checkered barbs (iridescent barb), gouramis or climbing fish, *Badis Badis*, and *Trichogaster* species.

The best, however, is a well planted species tank (25-gallon size containing three pairs of fish).

**Breeding:** Easy, a well planted 2 ½-gallon tank is sufficient. But provide hiding places for the female! Males occasionally

Courting male *Betta smaragdina*, the Emerald Betta, in a photo by the author.

*Betta splendens* REGAN, 1910

| | | | | | |
|---|---|---|---|---|---|
| 6/5 cm | 26/28° C | I/II | H1 | Z1 | A 1 |
| D I-II/7-10 | | A II-V/21-26 | | | mLR 27-32 |

A short-finned, wild-type *Betta splendens*. These fish are used for fighting. Photo by the author.

construct nests in holes (flowerpots), most, however, are at the water's surface.

During the spawning the female waits patiently under the nest. A spawning bout lasts up to about 20 to 30 embraces, during which at times 1 to 14 snow-white, bean-shaped eggs appear. After termination of the spawning act remove the female. The fry hatch after about 40 hours, hanging at first with their cement gland located on the head under the bubblenest and to water plants in the nest area. When they are first free swimming, one should take the father out.

Young should at first be fed with *Paramecium*, etc:, After about a week newly hatched brine shrimp. Breeding is not hard.

## *Betta splendens* Regan, 1910

SIAMESE FIGHTING FISH; BETTA.

**Systematics**: First description in "The Asiatic fishes of the family Anabantidae," in *Proc. Zool. Soc.* London, p. 782.

Previously erroneously designated *pugnax*, then often as *trifasciata* or *rubra*.

**splendens** (Latin): shining, glorious, splendid.

**Description**: Males larger, with more pronounced finnage, and usually more colorful. Females often show their white genital papilla. The wild form (called in Thailand *Lugk Tung* or children of the rice paddies) is thicker-set than the other bubblenest-building

*Bettas* and is in this respect very different from the otherwise very similar *Betta imbellis*. Round dorsal and caudal fins. Body scales of the otherwise dark males glisten blue when the light is just right. Usually one or two red stripes on the gill covers.

**Distribution**: Regan (1910) reports they are found in the area around Bangkok and the island of Penang, and then generalizes to include Thailand and the Malay Peninsula. The original area of this species may well be limited to the lowlands associated with the Menam and Mekong. My own re-investigation of Regan's *Bettas* from Penang revealed that they were *B. imbellis*. Other *Betta "splendens,"* too, reported from the peninsula turned out upon closer study to be *Betta imbellis* in each case. Among several hundred wild *Bettas* which I captured in all parts of Malaysia, I didn't find a single *Betta splendens*.

Wild *Betta splendens* live in thickly overgrown ponds and in only very slowly flowing waters. First introduced into France in 1874 (no breeding). First bred successfully by Jeunet from *Betta splendens* imported into France in 1892. Of these, two pairs reached J. Reichelt in Germany in 1892, who passed them on to a Moscow aquarist. From there, P. Matte brought progeny to Germany in the summer of 1893.

**Maintenance**: Best by pairs with other, not too lively fish. More than one male can be housed in large, well planted tanks, but there is the potential danger that the fish will get at each other. No special water or dietary needs. No water movement.

**Breeding**: Feed breeding fish well with live food.

Introduce by pairs in not too small a tank with hiding spots for the female. The proverbial aggressivness of the fish has to do with rivals for the territory. They treat their females, however, much less roughly than do many other labyrinth fishes. The females know how to ward off the attacks of their males by lowering their heads (away from the nest), making wiggling-swinging movements as well as taking on a special coloration (dark with three light transverse stripes).

Just like many bubblenest labyrinth fish, *Betta splendens* lay opaque white eggs that are heavier than water and sink to the bottom. In an emergency, the females can rear the brood, for example, if the male is removed from the tank.

The first two to three days after swimming free, the young feed on infusoria, then *Artemia*, and finally later, finely chopped *Tubifex*.

This green female *Betta* has finnage similar to that of the wild male on the facing page. Photo by A. van den Nieuwenhuizen.

Young males should be isolated as soon as possible (say, in mason or jam jars), otherwise they could inflict difficult-to-heal fin damage upon one another. They are easily recognized by their larger dorsal fin and more drawn-out anal fin tip.

**Breeding strains**: All strains are bred and, except for the fighters, also kept as described above. They come in the most varied colors and color combinations, usually in association with veil-like lengthening of the fins. These veiled fighting fish are among the most favorite aquarium fish.

Unfortunately, all *Betta splendens* are short-lived. They have already reached their peak vitality at four or five months of age. They rarely live more than a year.

**Fighting fish** have been bred for competitive fighting for centuries. They are terribly aggressive, bullishly thickset, have larger mouths and heads than the wild forms, and have shorter caudal fins. They attack blindly, even fish that are clearly more than a match for them, such as their predatory enemies. So, escaped specimens don't have any chance of survival in open water, and the danger of interbreeding with wild *Betta splendens* populations is minimal (according to D. Schaller).

**Veiled fighting fish** first appeared in Germany in the 1920's. According to Menzelmann (*Das Aquarium* p. 186, 1931), they came from a Chinese dealer in Bangkok, who was said to have gotten them from the Chinese in Singapore.

**Sail fin or Butterfly fighting fish** are characterized by a split caudal fin. Both sexes have an increased number of rays in the dorsal fin. The dorsal fin thus runs almost as long along the body as does the anal fin.

*Betta splendens* male.

*Betta taeniata* REGAN, 1910

| | | | | | |
|---|---|---|---|---|---|
| 8-6 cm | 25/27 °C | I/II | H1 | Z1 | A3 |
| D I/8 | | A II/20-22 | | | mLR 28-29 |

*Betta taeniata*. Photo by the author

## *Betta taeniata* Regan, 1910

BANDED FIGHTING FISH

**Systematics**: "The Asiatic fishes of the family Anabantidae." *Proc. Zool. Soc. London,* p. 781.

Recently, various species have been incorrectly identified as *B. taeniata:* All species designated *taeniata* before 1988 in aquarium books really belong to another species!

**taeniata** (Latin): with bands, banded.

**Description:** Sexes not always distinguishable: Females more heavyset and smaller.

Reminiscent of *B. picta* in habit, but larger. A conspicuous black spot at the base of the tail, separated from the dark bands that extend the length of the body. The black band may disappear, leaving the body a uniform red-brown color. Unpaired fins with conspicuous light blue border. Two light blue, shiny spots on the gill covers may appear in both sexes. Tail fin not extended, even in the male.

**Occurrence:** Southern Sarawak (western Borneo) in slow-moving streams in virgin forest. Not especially numerous.

First imported in August, 1988, by Dr. Jörg Vierke, at Husum, West Germany.

**Care:** Likes plants, sometimes quarrelsome with others of its species. Undemanding and does well in community tanks.

**Breeding:** Mouthbrooder, spawns even in community tanks. Courtship behavior as in *B. pugnax.* The males are, as a rule, reliable caretakers; as soon as the fry are free-swimming, they feed on small *Artemia* nauplii. Raising the young presents no problems.

*Betta unimaculata* (POPTA, 1906)

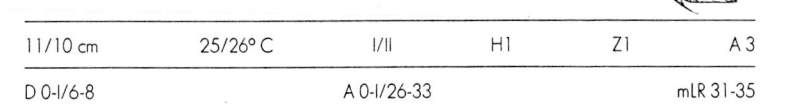

| | | | | | |
|---|---|---|---|---|---|
| 11/10 cm | 25/26° C | I/II | H1 | Z1 | A 3 |
| D 0-I/6-8 | | A 0-I/26-33 | | | mLR 31-35 |

# *Betta unimaculata* (Popta, 1906)

ONE-SPOT BETTA.

**Systematics**: First described in *Notes Leyden Mus.* 27, p. 10 as *Parophiocephalus unimaculata.* The attempt to reintroduce the old genus name was incorrect and unconvincingly founded. *B. ocellata* is a synonym.

**unimaculata** (Latin): with one spot.

**Description**: Males have large gold-shining scales under the eyes and on the gill covers. Elongated fish with distinctly large mouth, short-rayed anal fin and large, rounded caudal fin. Often has dark longitudinal stripes beginning directly at the pectoral fin and ending as a distinct dark spot at the root of the tail. Male in color is dark with bright golden green shining body scales.

**Distribution**: A common fish in all of northern Borneo, usually as a loner hidden among plants and undergrowth hanging into the water along banks. Prefers flowing water between 77° and 80.6° F. Even lives in sewage ditches. Linke measured a pH of 7.5 and conductivity of 80 microsiemens. First introduced by Horst Linke in April, 1980.

**Maintenance**: Hardy and easy in respect to water and diet. Because of the size, however, the tank or tank-mates should not be too small. Occasionally both male and female threaten with jaws agape, but biting hardly ever occurs.

Omnivorous, requiring a large amount of food, especially small and moderately sized worms.

**Breeding**: Mouthbrooders whose breeding is easy when done with well fed pairs. Spawning usually occurs in the evening.

The One-spot Betta, *Betta unimaculata*, common in northern Borneo. The fish shown is a male. Photo by the author.

The wild form of the Kissing Gourami, *Helostoma temminckii.* Photo by B. Kahl.

Mating as for the other mouthbrooding *Bettas* (see *B. picta*), except that the female swims away after laying the eggs, leaving the male to gather them up alone. At 77°F the young are released in nine days, and measure 0.24 inch (*picta* is 0.28 inch). They immediately feed on freshly hatched *Artemia* nauplii, and then grow rapidly.

## Genus *Helostoma* (Kuhl and Van Hasselt, 1829)

KISSING GOURAMI.

**Number of Species**: 1

**Systematics**: First described by Cuvier in *Le regne animal*, Vol. 2, p. 288.

**Helostoma:** from *holos* (Greek): ornamental nail, hump, wart; *stoma* (Greek): mouth, snout.

**Subfamily** Helostominae

**Distribution**: Indo-China, Malay Peninsula and Indonesia.

## *Helostoma temminckii* Cuvier and Valenciennes, 1831

KISSING GOURAMI, GREEN KISSER

**Systematics**: First described in *Hist. nat. Poiss.* VII, p. 341.

**Synonyms:** *H. servus, H. tambakkan, H. oligocanthum*, as well as the xanthistic forms *H. rudolfi* and *H. xanthoristi.*

**temminckii:** after the Dutch physician C. J. Temminck.

**Description**: In open waters, the maximal size of 11.8 inches is reached only in exceptional cases. Sexually mature fish are usually at least 4 1/2 inches long.

Sexually mature females can be

*Helostoma temminckii* CUVIER und VALENCIENNES, 1831

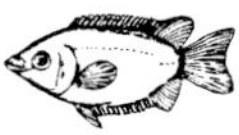

| | | | | | |
|---|---|---|---|---|---|
| ca. 20 cm | 26/29° C | I/II | H2/3 | Z3 | A 1 |

| | | |
|---|---|---|
| D XVI-XVIII/13-16 | A XIII-XV/17-19 | mLR 43-48 |

The usual aquarium variety of the Kissing Gourami, *Helostoma temminckii*. Photo by Jaroslav Elias.

identified by their greater body fullness. The anal fin of the male terminates more steeply to the rear, while the female's is uniformly rounded.

Oval, compressed body with pointed snout. Fleshy lips set with several rows of small, movable teeth. The rest of the oropharyngeal area is, in contrast to all other anabantoids, toothless. The gill structure has been converted to a highly developed filtering device which splendidly facilitates feeding on plankton.

**Distribution**: Central and southern Thailand, Malay Peninsula, Sumatra, Java, Borneo, in slowly moving waters, more frequently in the lush vegetation of ponds and lakes, swampy puddles and flooded land.

A favorite food fish bred and raised on large fish farms in many places, just as we farm carp.

First introduced in 1924 by Schult, Hamburg.

**Maintenance**: A problem fish to feed because it's a plankton feeder. Well acclimated fish are prodigious eaters that are always hungry. In the aquarium, prefers dry food directly from the water's surface, or *Cyclops* nauplii. No special water needs. Aquarium should not be under three feet long, and should be planted with Java fern and other hardy plants. Delicate plants take a beating. Relatively tolerant among themselves; don't introduce fast feeders as food competitors.

**Breeding**: Feed with live small

crustaceans (also *Artemia* nauplii). Introduce as pairs in tanks three feet long and up. Warm water temperature, otherwise other water values unimportant. Floating plants and floating stems of water plants to close off the surface of the water. Adults do not build nests. Following intensive "kissing," mating occurs in various places in the tank. Up to 10,000 eggs per spawning phase. The spawn is sticky and remains partially hanging from the water plants. The eggs float to the surface.

Some parents eat their own spawn, so scoop out the spawn or remove the parents after spawning. Eggs hatch after one day. Give powdered food after they swim free, then *Artemia* nauplii after one week.

**Color forms**: There is a gray-green form with a dark transverse stripe on the tail root, presumably the original form. Their dorsal and anal fins are darkly edged. Reported from the Bung Borapet lake in Thailand, among other places. The xanthistic form is uniformly pink or flesh colored, and is supposed to come originally from Java. Commercially you can also obtain light gray mixed forms without darkly edged fins.

**Comments**: Kissing gouramis are often seen engaged in their harmless mouth fights whereby they stand opposite each other and repeatedly press their lips together. This behavior is also part of the courtship ritual and can then be considered outright kissing!

A scientific style of drawing of the wild Kissing Gourami, *Helostoma temminckii.*

## Genus *Macropodus* Lacepede, 1802

PARADISE FISHES.

**Number of Species**: 3

**Systematics**: First described in *Hist. nat. Poiss.* III, pp. 416-417.

The group of small macropodes (spike-tailed paradise fish) limited to southern India and Sri Lanka was placed in its own genus *Pseudosphromenus* (Bleeker, 1879) based upon anatomical and behavioral characteristics (Vierke, 1975).

**Synonyms**: *Polyacanthus, Macropus*

**Macropodus:** from *makros* (Greek): large; *podos* (Greek): for foot or fin. So large fin.

**Subfamily** Macropodinae

**Distribution**: East and Southeast China, Korea, Vietnam, Taiwan, Borneo.

## *Macropodus chinensis*, (Bloch, 1790)

ROUND-TAILED PARADISE FISH.

**Systematics**: First described in *Naturgesch. auslaend. Fische*, Plate CCXVIII, Figure 1, as *Chaetodon chinesis.*

**Synonyms**: *Polyacanthus chinensis, P. paludous, Macropodus opercularis (!), Macropodus ctenopsoides.*

**chinensis** (Latin): Chinese.

**Description**: Female smaller,

*Macropodus chinensis* (BLOCH, 1790)

| | | | | | |
|---|---|---|---|---|---|
| 8,5/7 cm | 20/28° C | I | H 1/2 | Z1/2 | A 3 |
| D XIV-XVIII/5-7 | | A XVIII-XX/9-12 | | | mLR 28-30 |

A very beautiful and hardy fish is the Round-tailed Paradise Fish, *Macropodus chinensis.* Photo by the author.

The Black Paradise Fish, *Macropodus concolor*. Photo by the author.

with weaker finnage, and fuller. Powerful fish with spreadable gill cover spots. Caudal fin rounded. During courtship, male is light with tiger-like transverse stripes on the head and anterior part of the body, with the rest of the body uniformly grayish black. Caudal fin boldly orange. An otherwise indistinctly rimmed bluish-green spot to the rear of the dorsal fin now shines blue-green.

**Distribution**: Eastern China, in the north as far as Korea in waters of every kind. Not uncommon.

First introduced in 1913 by K. Siggelkov (Hamburg) from Hankow. Reintroduced in 1983 by O. Naujokat after long unavailability to aquarists.

**Maintenance**: Relatively peaceful and very attractive fish that are better suited to the community tank than are the other macropode species. Not fussy about water or diet, but susceptible to *Oodinium* infection. Keep cool in the winter!

**Breeding**: Breed in pairs just as for the other macropodes, except that they are less productive. Courting males show characteristic "pelvic fin flapping," alternatively folded back and spread out.

## *Macropodus concolor* Ahl, 1937

BLACK PARADISE FISH

**Systematics**: First described in "New freshwater fish from the Indian and Malayan region," in *Zool. Anzeiger* 117–118 as *Macropodus opercularis concolor*. The description already published by Schreitmueller (1936) under the name *Macropodus opercularis* var. *spechti* (in *Das Aquarium*, p. 181) I consider as *nomen oblitum*!

The black paradise fish differ so much from *M. opercularis* in fin formula, color pattern, behavior and origin, that their status as a species is clearly assured. The fact that *M. concolor* and *M. opercularis* produce fertile offspring in captivity is no evidence against their status as a species.

**concolor** (Latin): uniformly colored, monotone.

*Macropodus concolor* AHL, 1937

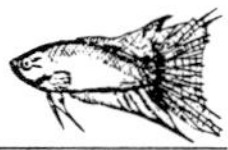

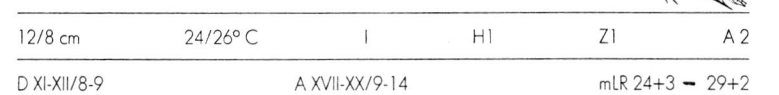

| | | | | | |
|---|---|---|---|---|---|
| 12/8 cm | 24/26° C | I | H1 | Z1 | A 2 |
| D XI-XII/8-9 | | A XVII-XX/9-14 | | mLR 24+3 – 29+2 | |

**Description**: Female has smaller fins. Female ready to spawn has lighter abdominal region.

Two-pointed caudal fin, no gill cover flecks. In the pet shop tank, they look plainly whitish. Acclimatized fish exhibit a reticular pattern on a monotonal gray ground, since each body scale is rimmed in black. Males are almost completely black during the spawning period, with red on the pelvic fins. Unpaired fins are edged in bluish white.

**Distribution**: Up to recently the species was believed to have originated in southern China or Vietnam, but no evidence could be shown for this belief. Just recently I received from H. Pinter four captured specimens from Sarawak (N.W. Borneo), and after studying them I was able to enlarge upon the description of the fin formula in the original description.

First introduction 1935.

**Maintenance**: Very easily satisfied. More peaceful than *M. opercularis*, but don't keep with very small tank-mates! Takes all kind of food.

**Breeding**: More aggressive at spawning time. Breed as pairs in a roomy tank. Water shouldn't be too hard! Very impressive courtship display when the male places himself diagonally before the female and spreads his huge, attractively marked caudal fin. Bubblenest builder. Reproductive behavior similar to that of *M. opercularis*. Young are easy to rear, but require better water quality than does *M. opercularis*.

## *Macropodus opercularis* Linné, 1758

PARADISE FISH.

**Systematics**: First described in *Systema naturae* 10th ed., p. 283 as *Labrus opercularis*.

The list of synonyms is impressive, so here's only a few: *Macropodus viridi-auratus, M. ocellatus, Platypodus furca, M.*

Paradise Fish, *Macropodus opercularis*, in a spawning embrace under their bubblenest. Photo by Burkhard Kahl.

*Macropodus opercularis* (LINNE, 1758)

| | | | | | |
|---|---|---|---|---|---|
| 11/8 cm | 23/26° C | I | H1/2 | Z1 | A 1 |
| D XIII-XVII/6-8 | | A XVII-XX/11-15 | | | mLR 28-31 |

*Macropodus opercularis*, the Paradise Fish. The male is the more colorful of the two. Photo by the author.

*venustus, M. filamentosus.*

**opercularis** (Latin): with gill cover (spot).

**Description**: Female is smaller, paler and with less developed finnage. Colorful bands over reddish-brown ground color, dark blue throat, acutely lengthened tip on dorsal and anal fins, with outside rays of the caudal fin lyrately prolonged.

**Distribution**: Eastern China and off-lying islands as far as the Ryukyus. Found in all standing and flowing waters as far as the tidal zone of the lowland rivers.

First introduced in 1869 into France.

**Maintenance**: This fish is easy on plants and easily satisfied in every way, although large spawning males could cause problems in community tanks, and become dangerous to their smaller tank-mates.

**Breeding**: Easy when done in pairs in not too small tanks. Provide hiding spots for the

female. Males build broad, flat bubblenest at the surface of the water. When mating, the male embraces his partner and gets her over on her back, with his head and caudal fin toward the bottom. After 14 seconds the eggs are released and the pair separates. The slightly milky opaque eggs rise and land in the bubblenest. The rapidity of development depends upon the water temperature. Rearing of the young is very easy.

**Comments**: There is a form with especially large blue parts. The top of the head and back of the male are predominantly grayish blue. It's still unclear whether this is a geographic race or a bred strain.

## Genus *Osphronemus* Lacepede, 1802

**GIANT GOURAMIS**

**Number of Species**: 1

**Systematics**: First described in *Hist. nat. Poiss.* III, p. 116.

The spelling *Osphromenus* is wrong.

**Osphronemus:** from *osphrome* (Greek) = scent sense, since Commerson, the original namer misinterpreted the labyrinth organ as a scenting adaptation.

## *Osphronemus goramy* Lacepede, 1802

GIANT GOURAMI

**Systematics**: First described in *Hist. nat. Poiss.* III, p. 117.

**Synonyms:** *Trichopus goramy, Osphromenus olfax, Trichopodus mentum, Trichopus satyrus, Osphromenus notatus*, and a few others.

**goramy**: from the trivial name used in the whole area of distribution.

**Description**: Fish of this species are among the largest fresh water aquarium fishes, but attain a length of "only" about 15 ¾ inches in exhibition tanks. The record length given in the data strip is hardly what can be expected from present-day fish production. The 39″ length was reported by Gill (1874) and referred to a specimen introduced as a young fish to the island of Martinique, where it attained the length of 39″ in 27 years. He reports further from the island of Bourbon, where a specimen reached a total length of 36″ and a height of 15″. Because of its thickly-set build, even "small" edible gouramis of 24-inch length (a sensational catch today!) weigh in at 12 to 14 pounds.

**Sexual differences:** Dorsal and anal fins of the male are somewhat pointed.

Young fish are graceful (occasionally confused with chocolate gouramis), relatively sharp-snouted with seven to ten dark transverse bands and a black, light-rimmed spot is at the root of the tail. Older specimens lack this marking and often have a thick head with jutting chin. Brown to bluish-gray coloration.

**Distribution**: Originally from the Indonesian-Malayan area, but is a favorite food fish in all southern Asia, as well as introduced into many other areas, including Australia (Victoria) and

*Osphronemus goramy* LACÉPÈDE, 1802

| | | | | | |
|---|---|---|---|---|---|
| bis 100 cm | 25° C | I/II | H2/3 | Z3 | A 2 |
| D XI-XIII/10-13 | | A IX-XII/16-22 | | | mLR 30-36 |

South America (Cayenne). Not choosey; lives in ponds, streams, ditches and large rivers as far as the brackish waters at their mouths.

First introduced in 1873 into France.

**Maintenance**: Young fish grow fast and are tolerant of their own kind. They are often plant eaters! Older specimens are much more portly and in really (!) large tanks go well as part of a community. Welcomed as exhibition specimens in large aquaria.

Voracious eaters who are not fussy about the water or diet.

**Breeding**: Up to now rarely bred in aquaria. (First bred in 1876 by Carbonnier, Paris). Reported to take on a deep black coloration and red eyes during brooding. The female lays batches of 15 to 20 eggs, which, in an aquarium, are stuck to rocks.

In their native habitat, they build spherical plant nests among bamboo stems. The nests are usually six to ten inches below the water's surface and about 12 inches above the bottom. The nests are spheroid, about six to 12 inches in diameter. The side facing the middle of the lake has about a four-inch opening. The male takes about eight to ten days to build a nest. Occasionally even double nests—two spheres, one above the other, with two openings.

Giant Gouramis, *Osphronemus goramy*. Photo by Burkhard Kahl.

Giant gouramis lay 500 to about 2000 floating eggs per spawning phase (strikingly few for these large fish, and explainable only by the intensive brood care), with the astonishingly large diameter of 2.7 to 2.9 mm (0.11 inch). The larvae are attentively guarded and only leave the nest in 15 to 18 days.

# Genus *Parosphromenus* Bleeker, 1879

LICORICE GOURAMIS

**Number of Species**: 5

**Systematics**: First described in *Verh. Akad. Amsterdam* XIX, *Mem. Poiss. pharyg. labyrinth*, p. 20. Closely related to *Malpulutta*.

**Parosphromenus:** from *par* (Greek prefix) for beside, false, deviating; *Osphromenus*, incorrect spelling of *Osphronemus*, giant gourami.

**Subfamily** Macropodinae

**Distribution**: Malay Peninsula and Indonesia.

**Comment**: All colorful dwarf gouramis can get by solely with their gill respiration, so don't have to use their labyrinth organ. They are sensitive to *very* sensitive wards, of which really only P. *filamentosus* and *P. paludicola* can be recommended for aquarists.

## *Parosphromenus* deissneri (Bleeker, 1859)

LICORICE GOURAMI.

**Systematics**: First described in *Nat. Tijdschr. Ned. Indie* XVIII, p. 376 as *Osphromenus deissneri.*

**Synonym:** *Polyacanthus deissneri*

**deissneri:** after a proper name.

**Description**: Sexual differentiation in normal coloration is not easy. Females are fuller, usually smaller and less intensively colored. Graceful fish with two bold dark stripes on an ochre ground. Underparts of courting males are dark. Light intervals about the width of the stripes. Light-colored back. Rounded caudal fin. Courting males show dark margins and bases of pelvic fins.

**Distribution**: Malay Peninsula, Sumatra, Bangka (*locus typicus*). Hidden in thickly overgrown, not too fast-flowing waters. Fish introduction uncertain, thus the longtime confusion with *Pseudosphromenus dayi.*

**Maintenance**: A peaceful, delicate fish that is suitable only for the species tank, with root hideaways or rock caves, and not too thick a vegetation (for then the fish would hardly leave their hideouts). Soft, slightly acidic water (peat filter) and pond food.

**Breeding**: Best bred in sterile aquarium (that is, no bottom materials or rooted plants) with some floating water sprite and flower-pot caves. Breed as pairs. Soft and slightly acidic water, always filtered, but without too strong a current.

Spawning occurs as with *P. filamentosus*. The eggs hatch in about 45 hours and the fry are free-swimming in another five days. First food: infusoria, and, after three to four days, freshly hatched *Artemia* nauplii.

## *Parosphromenus filamentosus* Vierke, 1981

SPIKE-TAILED LICORICE GOURAMI.

**Systematics**: First described in "*Parosphromenus filamentosus* n. sp. from southeast Borneo," in *Senckenbergiana biol.* 363-367.

**filamentosus** (Latin): with a thread, referring to the threadlike projection or extension of the caudal fin.

**Description**: Sexual differentiation in normal coloration is difficult. Female fuller, less intensively colored, with shorter caudal fin threads.

Graceful fish with two bold,

*Parosphromenus deissneri* (BLEEKER, 1859)

| | | | | | |
|---|---|---|---|---|---|
| 3,6/3,2 cm | 25/27° C | II | H2 | Z3 | A 3 |
| D X-XIII/5-8 | | A XI-XIII/6-10 | | | mLR 28 – 31+1 |

*Parosphromenus filamentosus* male in his breeding cave. Photo by the author.

dark longitudinal stripes on the body from the eye to the root of the tail. The middle stripe of the caudal fin is usually undivided and lengthened threadlike in adults of both sexes. Thread is black, and can extend up to 4mm (0.16 inch) beyond the spread caudal fin.

Males in color have darkly bordered unpaired fins. Otherwise, dorsal and caudal fins, as well as the back, are golden. Pelvic fins are shining blue.

**Distribution**: Southeastern Borneo, region around Bandjarmasin in various, slowly flowing waters (often drainage ditches). Not uncommon. The water there is brownish but clear (pH 5.2, conductivity 120 microsiemens, DH 2.8) with temperatures about 80.4°F.

First introduced in 1979 by A. Hanrieder and Hudoro.

*Parosphromenus filamentosus* VIERKE, 1981

| | | | | | |
|---|---|---|---|---|---|
| 3,6/3 cm | 25/28° C | II | H2 | Z2 | A 3 |
| D XII-XIII/6-7 | | A XI-XII/10 | | | mLR 29-30 |

**Maintenance**: Not fussy about water values, but delicate, so not for large community tank. Mini-tank. Likes to live hidden in plants. Seldom observed, however, if vegetation is too thick. Courting males are lively and colorful. Live food. Long-lived for small labyrinth fish; they live to be about three years old. Susceptible, however, to *Oodinium* infections.

**Breeding**: A few young fish in the species tank occasionally grow large. Breeding by pairs, as for *P. deissneri*, is better. Mating occurs in the cave. Following the laying of eggs, the male slowly opens his embrace and releases his mate, but remains there suspended in the water. The milky opaque eggs rest on his curved body and on the anal fin as if on a tray or in a bowl. The female now takes the spawn and swims with it in her mouth up to the nest, where she sticks it into the bubbles. No more spawn remains for the male to gather as he comes to from his mating trance. Mating is repeated about every ten minutes. In about three hours the female leaves the brood cave. Further brood care falls to the male. At 77°F the larvae hatch in about 48 hours. They are milky white and hang like little commas among the frothy bubbles.

For rational breeding, the eggs should be siphoned out following spawning. I have counted up to 120 eggs, but there are seldom more than 50. Transfer the spawn to 2-quart jars along with water from the breeding tank and disinfect with some potassium permanganate (small pinch). Aerate (not too vigorously).

After the young swim free, turn off the aeration and feed with infusoria. In three days give freshly hatched *Artemia* nauplii. Convert as soon as possible to rotifers and *Daphnia*, for exclusive feeding with *Artemia* repeated for more than several weeks leads to mass death.

## *Parosphromenus nagyi* Schaller, 1985

NAGY'S LICORICE GOURAMI.

**Systematics**: First described in "*Parosphromenus nagyi* spec. nov., a new colorful gourami from Malaysia (preliminary report)" in DATZ 301–303. The fish description did not include any definite information on scale or fin ray counts, or proportional values (ratios), or size of the specimens. Types are absent.

**Description**: The species is distinguished from the closely related *P. deissneri* in its different display coloration, behavior (Schaller) and its larger eyes. Otherwise there are no differences in the morphometric or meristic values (information on scales counts, fin ray counts, ratios) according to my own studies.

Males without red. Ground color dark bluish-gray, with two light gray longitudinal stripes, both starting at the rear edge of the eye, and the upper one ending at the root of the tail. Display color almost black. Round caudal fin.

**Distribution**: In the eastern and western Malay Peninsula, in springwater rivers of the lowland rainforest. They inhabit the very slowly moving, overgrown waters,

or those enriched with fallen foliage. They often form loose schools here and frequently form communities with *Betta coccina*. (See under *B. coccina* for such a location at Rawang, with water characteristics).

**Maintenance**: Peaceful, delicate fish. Provide root hideaways, rock caves and water somewhat longer drawn-out pelvic fins. Delicate fish whose dorsal fin is larger than the other *Parosphromenus* species. Two dark longitudinal stripes on cream-colored ground color. Caudal fin pointed in older specimens. Male golden brown in display coloration, with reddish longitudinal stripes during courtship.

*Parosphromenus nagyi* SCHALLER, 1985

| | | | | | |
|---|---|---|---|---|---|
| ca. 3 cm | 26/28° C | II | H2 | Z2 | A 3 |

*Parosphromenus paludicola* TWEEDIE, 1952

| | | | | | |
|---|---|---|---|---|---|
| 3,7/3,3 cm | 25/27° C | II | H2 | Z2 | A 3 |
| D XVII-XVIII/6-7 | | A XIV-XV/7-8 | | mLR 26-27 (+2 – 3) | |

plants, but also sufficient swimming room. Soft, lightly acidic water (peat filter).

**Breeding**: These fish are easy to breed. Precise information is published in *Das Aquarium* (1988) by Dr. Vierke. This species is not essentially different from *deissneri* or *filamentosus*.

## *Parosphromenus paludicola* Tweedie, 1952

SWAMP LICORICE GOURAMI.

**Systematics**: First described in "Notes on Malayan Freshwater Fishes" in *Bull. Raffl. Mus.* 24, 69-71.

**paludicola** (Latin): swamp inhabitant.

**Description**: Sexual differentiation difficult. Males have

**Distribution**: Eastern part of the Malay Peninsula, in southern Thailand and Malaysia in the lowlands as well as in swamps of the central region. Type site is a forest swamp south of Merchang, Trengganu. Nagy reports for his site (a puddle-like residue of a ditch in a swampy area): a 78.8°F temperature and conductivity of 150 microsiemens. Linke reported a site at Kuala Brang: 78.8°F, 6 microsiemens, pH 5.5. The fish were living in shallow overgrown weedy spots in the shaded bank zone. First introduction by P. and T. Nagy of Salzburg, Austria, in May, 1977.

**Maintenance**: Peaceful fish, less sensitive than *P. deissneri*, but needs extra care in a special tank. Water should not be too hard. Light filtration without much water movement. Live food.

**Breeding**: Breed in pairs as with *P. deissneri*. Spawning behavior is similar by and large to that of *P. filamentosus*. Artificial breeding is usually resorted to for *P. deissneri* and *P. filamentosus*.

## *Parosphromenus parvulus* Vierke, 1979

LESSER LICORICE GOURAMI

**Systematics**: First described in "A new labyrinth fish from Borneo—*Parosphromenus parvulus* Nov. Spec." in *Das Aquarium* 247–250. Smallest hitherto known labyrinth fish species. The size, about 1¼ inches, refer to aquarium specimens. Such sizes are presumably not attained in the wild.

**parvulus** (Latin): Very small.

**Description**: Female has colorless fins. Delicate fish with two vaguely delimited dark longitudinal stripes which are, however, rarely discernible. Dark spot on the peripheral part of the soft-rayed dorsal fin. Rounded caudal fin.

Males in display color are smoky gray with broad, silver-gray longitudinal stripes on the body. Dorsal and caudal fins broadly edged in black, with large brilliant red parts in the middle portion of the fins.

**Distribution**: South Borneo. Typical site is the Mentaya River system about 150 miles northwest of Bandjarmasin. The species is, however, more widely distributed. Roberts has captured them in the Kapuas system, and Vogt somewhat north of there. Typical site is a dark, slowly flowing stream with acidic water (less than pH 4.8), 75.2°F (8 a.m.) and 75 microsiemens conductivity. There they inhabit the thick vegetation along the banks. First introduced in 1978 by E. Korthaus, Dr. W. Foersch and A. Hanrieder.

**Maintenance and Breeding**: Very sensitive fish that were first bred in 1988. Keep in small species tank with peat filtration, soft and acidic water. Change the water frequently. Feed small live food.

## Genus *Sphaerichthys* Canestrini, 1860

CHOCOLATE GOURAMIS (in the broad sense)

**Number of species:** 3 or 4 (if one can allow *Sphaerichthys selatanensis* species status).

**Systematics**: First described in *Verhandl. Zoo - bot. Gesellschaft*, Vienna X, p. 707.

**Sphaerichthys:** from *sphaera* (Greek): spheroid body; *ichthys* (Greek): fish.

*Parosphromenus parvulus* VIERKE, 1979

| | | | | | |
|---|---|---|---|---|---|
| 2,7/2,7 cm | 25° C | II | H3 | Z3 | A 3 |
| D X-XI/7 | | A VIII-IX/10-11 | | mLR 26+2 — 27+2 | |

*Sphaerichthys acrostoma* VIERKE, 1979

| | | | | | |
|---|---|---|---|---|---|
| 9/8,5 cm | 26/28° C | II | H2 | Z3 | A 3 |
| D VI/7-9 | A IX-X/19-21 | | mLR 26+4 – 28+3 | | |

**Subfamily**: Trichogasterinae. Assignment of this genus (just as *Parasphaerichthys*) to the subfamily Trichogasterinae (Liem, 1963) seems quite dubious to me, but as long as no detailed studies are available, it can stay there.

**Distribution**: Malaysia and Indonesia.

## *Sphaerichthys acrostoma* Vierke, 1979

SHARP-NOSED CHOCOLATE GOURAMI

**Systematics**: First described in "Description of a new species and a new subspecies of the genus *Sphaerichthys* from Borneo" in *Das Aquarium* pp. 339–343.

**acrostoma:** from *acro* (Greek): pointed, high; *stoma* (Greek): mouth.

**Description**: Female somewhat stocky, with concave throat (usually bulges somewhat). Gill cover bands bolder in females.

Small-mouthed fish with long, pointed snout. Characteristic head markings. Light gray-brown body ground color. Often vague, interrupted stripes on belly. Forked caudal fin.

**Distribution**: Southern Borneo in the Mentaya region (150 miles northwest of Bandjarmasin) on grassy overgrown river banks. Water values: 0 hardness, 20 microsiemens conductivity at 89.6°F, pH 7.6 (!).

*S. osphromenoides*, on the other hand, was found only in acidic waters, which are much more common in the same area.

First introduction in 1978 by Dr. Foersch, E. Korthaus and A. Hanrieder.

**Maintenance and Breeding**: Keep in well planted species tank. Soft but not acidic water. Fine living foods.

Breeding unsuccessful up to now. Dr. Foersch observed that males (?) are mouthbrooders. Unfortunately their throat sacks or gullets were empty again in two days' time.

The Sharp-nosed Chocolate Gourami, *Sphaerichthys acrostoma*. This is a very rarely seen fish even though it is fairly plentiful in Borneo. Photo by Dr. Walter Foersch.

*Sphaerichthys osphromenoides* CANESTRINI, 1860

| | | | | | |
|---|---|---|---|---|---|
| 6/5,5 cm | 28/30° C | I/II | H3 | Z3 | A 1 |
| D (VIII) IX-XI (XII) / 7-10 | | A (VII) VIII-X / 18-22 | | | mLR 26-30 |

Chocolate Gouramis, *Sphaerichthys osphromenoides*. These magnificent fish are among the most gentle of all aquarium fishes. They are also very shy and difficult to breed. Photo by Burkhard Kahl.

# *Sphaerichthys osphromenoides* Canestrini, 1860

CHOCOLATE GOURAMI

**Systematics**: First described in *Verhand. Zool. - Bot. Gesellschaft* Vienna X, p. 707.

**Synonym**: *Osphromenus malayanus*

**osphromenoides:** gourami-like.

**Description**: Males larger, with better developed and somewhat pointed dorsal fin. Female has weaker margins on the anal fin. Oval body form, laterally very compressed. Small mouth. Dark brown with three to four transverse stripes. Rarely with a longitudinal stripe. Forked caudal fin.

**Distribution**: Southern part of the Malay Peninsula, Sumatra, and southern part of Borneo. In weedy overgrown shallow puddles and ditches, preferably in slowly flowing streams, often with dark brown water. The water is always soft and acidic (pH 4.6 to 6.5), with temperatures between 78.8° and 89.6°F.

**Maintenance**: Keep in a species aquarium! In normal community tanks, chocolate gouramis are usually earmarked for death. They are susceptible to *Oodinium*. Proper care requires water that is soft, acidic (pH about 6), very clean and slightly moving

(peat filter with not too powerful a rotary pump), and a relatively high temperature. The tank should contain at least 25 gallons (more is better) and be well planted. Make regular partial water changes! Pond food. Under these conditions, chocolate gouramis are well maintained and reproduce.

**Breeding**: These fish spawn in the species tank. The females are mouthbrooders. The male helps with the eggs (laid on the bottom) by spitting them over to the female. The young are released after 17 to 19 days (at 80.6°F), at which time they are already chocolate brown, except for a yellowish, transparent ring at the middle of the body. They now have an average total length of 6.7mm (0.26 inch) and immediately feed on *Artemia* nauplii (Linke, 1983). A month later the young chocolate gouramis measure an average length of 12 mm (0.47 inches) and 5 mm (0.2 inches) height. The young like current. According to field observations (Schaller), they prefer to school in rapidly flowing stream and canal sections just below the surface of the water.

The notion, long held to be erroneous, that chocolate gouramis also care for their spawn in bubblenests under certain conditions, has been verified recently by Swedish aquarists (J.E. Larsonn, personal communication, 1983).

**Comment**: There is a chocolate gourami in southeastern Borneo (Kalimantan Selatan), that differs in several respects from the normal one: fewer spines in the dorsal fin (only VII), form and size of the gill cover, somewhat smaller head and different coloration. The most characteristic differences in coloration are a light longitudinal stripe running along at the base of the anal fin, and another light, longitudinal stripe from the eye to the upper (forward) attachment of the anal fin. There are differences, too, in the number of transverse stripes. This form was described as a subspecies, *Sph. osphromenoides selatanensis* (Vierke, 1979). Tyson R. Roberts considers it, however, as a separate species, which would then be called *Sphaerichthys selatanensis*.

## *Sphaerichthys vaillanti* (Pellegrin, 1930)

VAILLANT'S CHOCOLATE GOURAMI.

**Systematics**: First described in "Description of a new Anabantidae fish from Borneo, belonging to the genus *Sphaerichthys*" in *Bull. Soc. Zool. France.* Paris pp. 242-244.

**vaillanti:** from M. Leon Vaillant, who first described the species in 1893, but considered it *Ctenops nobilis*.

*Sphaerichthys vaillanti* PELLEGRIN, 1930

D VII-VIII/7-8 | A IX-XI/16-18 | mLR 27-29

**Description**: Similar to *Sph. acrostoma* in body form, but mouth stubbier, eyes larger. About nine bold dark stripes on the lower part of the body. A light, variously interrupted longitudinal stripe runs from the upper margin of the gill cover towards the rear, ending as a distinct, dark-rimmed light spot at the root of the caudal fin (described from a preserved specimen).

**Distribution**: Sebroeang reported as the origin, apparently a tributary of the Kapuas River in southwestern Borneo.

This species has not yet been imported, and other specimens than those described by Vaillant have not been captured again to date.

## Genus *Trichogaster* Bloch, 1801

**Number of Species**: 4

**Systematics**: First described in Schneider, *Systema ichthyologiae*, p. 164.

**Synonyms**: *Trichopodus, Trichopus*

**Trichogaster:** from *trichias* (Greek): hairy; *gaster* (Greek): stomach, referring to the threadlike pelvic fins.

**Subfamily**: Trichogasterinae

**Distribution**: Indo-China and Indonesia

## *Trichogaster leerii* (Bleeker, 1852)

PEARL GOURAMI.

**Systematics**: First described in *Naturk. Tijdsch. Nederl.- Indie*, III, p. 577.

For a long while the species was not distinguished from *T. trichopterus*. The spelling of *leeri* (with one i) does not agree with the original description.

**leerii:** from the physician J. M. van Leer, a colleague of Bleeker.

**Description**: Female stockier. Male has longer dorsal fin and, when older, thready, greatly lengthened soft rays in the anal fin. More colorful. Body and unpaired fins with mosaic-like markings, shining like mother-of-pearl. Male in display coloration has orange to deep red throat and breast.

**Distribution**: South Borneo, Sumatra and in the south of the Malay Peninsula. Mosaic or pearl gouramis prefer the shallow, warm and overgrown parts of standing or slowly flowing waters.

Early reports that this species also occurs in Thailand ("Area around Bangkok not uncommon") as well as reports from Java are based presumably on mistaken identity.

First introduced in 1933 by Haertel (Dresden).

**Maintenance**: Very peaceful and easy on plants. Ideal for a quiet community tank. Tank should not be too small, and be well planted. Accepts dry food and live food which is not too coarse.

**Breeding**: Successful breeding depends very much upon the spirit of the breeding fish, in particular the spawning desire (and ability) of the female, good preliminary feeding with live foods, and increased temperature.

Breed in pairs in not too small a tank (from 32 inches length and up) which is planted to include floating species (Sumatra fern).

*Trichogaster leerii* (BLEEKER, 1852)

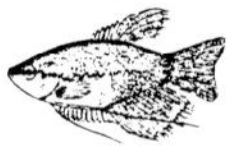

| | | | | | |
|---|---|---|---|---|---|
| 12/10 cm | 27/29° C | I | H1 | Z2 | A 1 |

| | | |
|---|---|---|
| D V-VII/8-10 | A XII-XIV/25-30 | mLR 44-50 |

Water should not be too hard. Don't disturb the breeding pair!

Males build a small bubblenest at first, then enlarge it as time passes, but without bringing in any plant matter. The female who is ready for spawning forces herself into the flank of the male, who is under the nest, until he wraps himself around her. They remain 20 to 25 seconds in this embrace, then the male turns the female over on her back, at which time the eggs are released. Then the male drives the female away and concentrates on the eggs. The light eggs rise up to the nest, but those which float about are collected by the male. Several hundred, often up to 2000 eggs are laid. At 82.4°F, the young hatch in about a day, and swim free in another two days. Now the father should be removed. Feed the young infusoria, then in four to eight days they can handle the smallest of *Artemia* nauplii.

**Comments**: Many *Trichogaster leerii* males occasionally spit grains of sand into their bubblenests. The sand drops down to the bottom, where it forms a pile. Such a "sandhill construction" can also be seen with *Colisa* males. It is often seen with isolated males after nestbreeding is over. I consider the inclusion of sand a substitute activity of males who are not caring for broods, but who are in a brooding mood ("dry run" behavior, Vierke, 1973).

The Moonlight Gourami, *Trichogaster microlepis.*

## *Trichogaster microlepsis* (Günther, 1861)

MOONLIGHT GOURAMI.

**Systematics**: First described in *Catalogue Fish. Brit. Mus.* III, p. 385.

**Synonyms:** *Trichopus*

*Trichogaster microlepis* (GÜNTHER, 1861)

| | | | | | |
|---|---|---|---|---|---|
| 18/15 cm | 27/29° C | I | H1 | Z2 | A 1 |

| | | |
|---|---|---|
| D III-IV/8-10 | A X-XI/34-40 | mLR 50-65 |

The Moonlight Gourami, *Trichogaster microlepis* in a spawning embrace. Photo by the author.

*parvipinnis* and *Deschauensee chryseus*.

**microlepis** (Latin): with small scales.

**Description**: Male has orange-colored pelvic threadfins. Threads on females are colorless to yellowish. Dorsal fin in the male is usually broader and somewhat longer.

Silvery, often with bluish-violet shimmer. Indented head profile (saddle-nose). Occasionally exhibits a dark longitudinal band beginning behind the head and ending in a boldly black spot at the root of the tail.

**Distribution**: Widely distributed in Cambodia and central Thailand, although rarer than *T. trichopterus* and *T. pectoralis*. They like to stay in standing or slowly flowing, heavily vegetated waters. A food fish in its native area.

First introduced in May, 1951, by the Hamburg Aquarium.

**Maintenance**: Very peaceful fish which are quite suitable for a large community tank, where they contrast well with colorful fishes. They need only quiet tank-mates. They accept dry food and live food which is not too coarse. No

*Trichogaster pectoralis* (REGAN, 1910)

| | | | | | |
|---|---|---|---|---|---|
| 20/18 cm | 25/29° C | I/II | H2 | Z2 | A 2 |
| D VII/10-11 | | A IX-XI/36-38 | | | mLR 55-63 |

special water requirements.

**Breeding**: Breed in pairs in well planted, undisturbed tanks not smaller than 32 inches along a side. Floating plants can include *Riccia.*

The male often builds a huge plant nest with the help of bubbles, and which sticks up out of the water like a dome. Watch out that the often very rough males don't harass the unreceptive females to death. During courtship, the male's bluish-violet shimmering body, red eyes and orange-red pelvic threadfins are quite attractive. Mating itself is rather quiet, directly under the nest, similar to *T. leerii.* Very productive. Easy to rear the young.

## *Trichogaster pectoralis* (Regan, 1910)

SNAKESKIN GOURAMI OR ZEBRA GOURAMI

**Systematics**: First described in "The fishes of the family Anabantidae." *Proc. Zoo. Soc.* London. p. 784 as *Trichopodus pectoralis.*

**Synonym:** *Osphromenus cantoris.*

**pectoralis** (Greek): refers to the large breast fins, the pelvics.

**Description:** A local strain in central Thailand is supposed to become significantly larger than the size given above (Smith). In the aquarium, they usually grow to only about 5". Males have a

The Snakeskin Gourami, *Trichogaster pectoralis.* This is a male. Photo by the author.

*Trichogaster trichopterus* (PALLAS, 1777)

| | | | | | |
|---|---|---|---|---|---|
| 15/13 cm | 24/28° C | I | H1 | Z1 | A 1 |
| D VI-VIII/8-10 | | A X-XII/33-38 | | | mLR 40-52 |

distinctly longer dorsal fin.

They are less compressed laterally than *T. leerii* and *T. microlepis*. Body elongated. Ground color gray. A dark, repeatedly interrupted longitudinal stripe runs from the eye to the root of the tail. Occasionally slanted transverse bands, especially on the hind part of the body, hence the occasional name Zebra Gourami.

**Distribution**: The original range is limited to the lowlands crossed by the lower courses of the Menam and Mekong. A favorite food fish now introduced to the Malay Peninsula (beginning of the 20th century), Sri Lanka, Haiti, northern Borneo (1949). Schaller observed them in Rangoon, Burma, too.

Frequent inhabitants of slowly moving and standing waters, they like flooded rice puddies. First introduced in 1896 by J.F.G. Umlauff, Hamburg.

**Maintenance**: Peaceful but quite shy fish which, despite their size, are suitable for well planted community tanks (not under 50 gallons). No special water or dietary requirements.

**Breeding**: Breed as pairs in large, well planted tanks (at least 20 gallons), in an as undisturbed a spot as possible. Bubblenest builders. Productive (3000 to 5000 eggs per spawning phase). No problems with rearing the young.

## *Trichogaster trichopterus* (Pallas, 1777)

THREE-SPOT GOURAMI, BLUE GOURAMI.

**Systematics**: First described in *Spicilegia zoologica*, part 8, p. 45 as *Labrus trichopterus.*

**Synonyms**: *Osphromenus siamensis, Trichopus siamensis, Trichopodus cantoria, Trichopus maculatus, Osphromenus salgonensis, Osphromenus insulatus.*

**trichopterus:** from *trichias* (Greek): hairy; *pteron, pteryx* (Greek): wing, fin. Hence "with hairy fins," referring to the pelvic fins.

**Description**: Males are slimmer with distinctly longer, somewhat pointed dorsal fin. Wild forms vary greatly depending upon origin. Two round black spots at the center of the body and the root of the tail are characteristic. Ground color is blue-green to yellow-brown. The body is marked with a variable

The Blue Gourami. Many different varieties have been produced in aquariums all over the world. This is one of the purest and most early of them. Photo by Andre Roth.

The 3-Spot Blue Gourami, *Trichogaster trichopterus.* Photo by H. J. Richter.

number of fine or coarse, but always irregular, wavy transverse bands. Round, orange or yellow spots mark the anal fin.

**Distribution**: In all Indo-China except Burma, in Indonesia east of Sumba, and in the northeast as far as the Philippines. In ponds, rice fields, lakes, drainage canals and rivers. Common everywhere. Prefers vegetated areas, even brackish water. First introduced in 1896 by J.F.G. Umlauff, Hamburg.

**Maintenance**: One of the hardiest of aquarium fish, which easily accepts any water and food. Well suited to a planted, not too small community tank, although the male can occasionally get rough, so if possible take only one male.

**Breeding**: Bubblenest builders. Breeding efforts are more successful than with other *Trichogaster* species, but the breeding tank should measure at least 24 inches along a side, and the female should be provided with sufficient hiding spots to avoid the occasionally very dogged pursuit of the male.

The male exhibits, just as the other *Trichogaster* species, "directional" swimming with widely spread fins and the raised tail ("hollow or small of the back"). The female initiates mating by biting precisely midway between both points. Other *Trichogaster* males begin immediately with the embrace, but *T. trichopterus* reacts peculiarly – the male lays back his dorsal fin, sinks down somewhat until the female is directly above him, and swims back and forth repeatedly as he rubs his back up against the belly of the female. This behavior can last a minute or longer; the subsequent embrace can last about 35 to 55 seconds. The young are easy to rear.

In large, well arranged breeding tanks, a large number of young fish can grow without parental assistance. The parents often turn out to be continuous spawners (that also applies to the other species of the genus), which spawn every few days. Then you have young fish at all stages of development, although that is not a rational method of breeding.

**Breed strains**: In maintenance and breeding, treat all color varieties as above. Color changes are due in part to withdrawal of a pigment from the process (a ground color) as well as to irregular accumulation of pigment (Cosby gourami). Withdrawal of pigments is due to genetic changes (mutation) which can occur in the wild (possibly in blue gouramis) as well as in breeding tanks.

**Blue gourami**: No yellow or dark transverse bands, occasionally side spots are absent, too. Presumably a mutant which occurs in nature, even in a circumscribed area of Sumatra. There is no definitive explanation. Ladiges described the form in 1933 as *Trichogaster trichopterus sumatranus*.

**Cosby gourami**: Bred strain that exhibits a few thick transverse bands and spots in a blue ground. Apparently first produced by the American breeder Cosby.

**Gold gourami**: Bred strain without blue. Here the color has

actually been withdrawn (that is, does not participate), whereas it is involved in the blue gourami. Cross-breeding of these two forms produces the natural brownish form as well as the "pure" forms. All indications are against the often expressed opinion that this form has been bred from the blue gourami. All other color strains, too, are apparently from the wild form.

**Silver gourami**: Silvery color-deficient mutant, which, because of its unattractiveness, is seldom available commercially. They keep appearing, though, during the breeding of gold gouramis.

**Comments**: Spotted gouramis and their color varieties are known as annihilators of planarians and hydra, but they only attack these unwelcomed guests after several days fasting.

*T. trichopterus* captured in the wild exhibit various colorations depending upon "mood," which can change very quickly. Females, for example, are all dark with bright (!) body spots just before spawning, but after the spawning act, that is, not even a minute later, they are again light gray with black spots.

## *Genus Trichopsis* Canestrini, 1860

CROAKING GOURAMIS (in the broad sense).

**Number of Species**: 3

**Systematics**: First described in *Verh. Zool. bot. Ges.* Vienna vol. 10, p. 702.

**Type species**: *Trichopsis striatus* Bleeker.

The genus was long ascribed to *Ctenops*.

**Trichopsis:** *Trichopus* - like (*Trichopus* is a synonym of *Trichogaster*)

**Subfamily**: Trichogasterinae

**Distribution**: Indo-China and Indonesia.

## *Trichopsis pumilus* (Arnold, 1936)

PYGMY GOURAMI.

**Systematics**: First described in *Wochenschr. Aquar. - Terrarienkd.* 33 as *Ctenops pumilus*.

The Pygmy Gourami, *Trichopsis pumilus*. Photo by the author.

*Trichopsis pumilus* (ARNOLD, 1936)

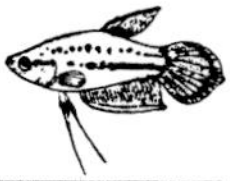

| | | | | | |
|---|---|---|---|---|---|
| 3,5/4,5 cm | 26/28° C | II | H1 | Z1 | A 2 |
| D III/7-8 | | A V/20-25 | | | mLR 27-28 |

*Trichopsis schalleri* LADIGES, 1962

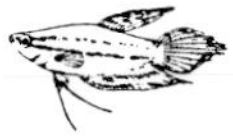

| | | | | | |
|---|---|---|---|---|---|
| 6/5,5 cm | 26/28° C | I/II | H1 | Z1 | A 2 |
| D III-IV/6-7 | | VIII-IX/19-22 | | | mLR 28-29 |

**pumilus** (Latin): pygmy.

**Description**: Males usually smaller. Females clearly identified by their often yellowish ovary which shows through under the scales. The ovary is best seen in cross-lighting when the fish is placed in a small glass container and held up against a bright light source. Body is pale yellow and shimmers turquoise when the light strikes. Two dark longitudinal stripes along the body, the upper of which, particularly, is broken up into single spots. The lower stripe runs from the eye to the root of the tail. The red eyes give off an iridescent blue. Unpaired fins are spotted.

**Distribution**: Definite finds are reported from central Thailand and around Saigon. They live in thickly overgrown, weedy standing waters at temperatures around 82.4°F. Requirements for purity of this pond do not seem to be too great.

Occasionally seen schooling together through the water.

First introduced in September, 1913 by Scholze and Ploetzschke (Berlin).

**Maintenance**: Ideal fish for small, well planted tanks; in usual community tanks, however, they do not survive. Suitable tank-mates are *Colisa sota*, hatchetfish or small killies. Croaking gouramis take dry food, but naturally prefer live food of all kinds. Can be kept and bred in rather hard water.

**Breeding**: Breed in pairs in planted tank which measures at least 12 inches along a side. The male builds his nest preferentially in a cave at ground level, often under the leaf of a floating plant, of a *Cryptocoryne* or in the roots of a Sumatra fern.

Mating occurs secretively and is often overlooked. The embrace lasts only about two seconds at a time. Initiation of mating, in contrast to that of the gouramis, is by the female, who places herself diagonally in front of the male; he swims into her flank and she lets herself be embraced. The opaque milky sinking eggs appear in clumps, and not separately as with labyrinth fish of other genera. The male can thus snap up the whole clump with a single, lightning-fast gulp and carry them into the nest.

One spawning phase produces only 100 to 300 eggs, which the male cares for alone. The females usually remain near the nest and help the male in defending the periphery of the territory. The young hatch (at 80.6°F) in 42 to 46 hours and swim free in another two days. In a month, the young can attain a total length of 0.8 inch, and can be ready to spawn in two months.

During courtship, the males can produce croaking sounds, which are accompanied by vibrating pectoral fins. In contrast

to other *Trichopsis* species, *T. pumilus* females cannot croak. However, the males' approximately one-third more powerfully developed sound musculature allows them to croak almost ten times as loudly as the almost ten times as heavy *T. vittatus* (Krotochvil, 1980).

## *Trichopsis schalleri* Ladiges, 1962

THREE-STRIPED CROAKING GOURAMI.

**Systematics**: First described in "*Trichopis schalleri* spec. nov. a new gourami from Thailand."*DATZ*, pp. 101–103.

*T. schalleri* is very closely related to *T. vittatus*, yet we are probably dealing with two separate species. *T. schalleri* is apparently not identical with the *Trichopsis harrisi* described by Fowler, either.

**schalleri:** from D. Schaller, discoverer of this fish.

**Description**: Sexual differentiation is most successful with the crosslighting technique described for *T. pumilus. T. schalleri* males are somewhat larger than the females.

Two longitudinal stripes, both beginning at the rear margin of the eye and ending at the root of the tail; the upper stripe becomes indistinct at times.

The caudal fin is pointed. Very similar to *T. pumilus* in coloration, but that fish's stripes are larger.

**Distribution**: Thailand. Schaller captured the type specimens in the Nam-Mun region near Korat. Linke's were further north between Khon Kaen and Nong Khai in rice fields, swampy meadows, and klongs (canals), often together with *T. vittatus* and *Betta smaragdina.*

First introduced in 1961 by D. Schaller.

**Maintenance**: A peaceful fish that does not destroy plants, but which shouldn't be kept with overly rough fish. Unpretentious, but occasionally needs live food.

**Breeding**: Not difficult when bred in pairs. Interbreeds with *T. vittatus*, which it very much resembles in reproduction.

## *Trichopsis vittatus* (Cuvier and Valenciennes, 1831)

CROAKING GOURAMI.

**Systematics**: First described in *Histoire naturelle des poissons*, vol. 7, pg. 387 as *Osphromenus vittatus.*

A variable, very widely distributed species.

**Synonyms**: *Trichopus striatus, Ctenops vittatus, Trichopsis harrisi.*

**vittatus:** (Latin): banded.

**Description**: Male has large-

*Trichopsis vittatus* (CUVIER und VALENCIENNES, 1831)

| | | | | | |
|---|---|---|---|---|---|
| 7/6,5 cm | 26/28° C | I | H1 | Z1 | A 2 |
| D II-IV/6-8 | | A VI-IX/19-28 | | | mLR 28-29 |

*Trichopsis schalleri* servicing its eggs. Photo by H. J. Richter.

surfaced fins. Most reliable sexual differentiation is with the translucent method. (See *T. pumilus*).

Slender fish with short dorsal fin set way back. Caudal fin drawn out very long, often in several ways. Head profile usually deeply saddle-like (but not the specimens from Borneo I examined). Very variable markings depending upon origin. Usually three, occasionally two or four dark partially not coordinated longitudinal stripes along the body. Body is brownish in life, though iridescent greenish or blue, often violet. Unpaired fins are reddish, violet or bluish. Iris shining light blue, rimmed in red.

**Distribution**: One of the most common labyrinth fish in Indo-China and Indonesia. It was reported to have been captured on the island of Banda itself, not far from Ceram and New Guinea.

*Trichopsis vittatus* is a fish of standing or only slowly moving waters, where it is found chiefly in overgrown marginal areas. It does not inhabit ponds as thickly overgrown, though, as does *Betta splendens*, so the two areas are largely mutually exclusive. Not fussy in water requirements, and is even found in the *klongs* (canals) of Bangkok.

First introduced in 1899 by H. Stueve of Hamburg.

**Maintenance**: A fish which is satisfied even with relatively unfavorable water conditions. Peaceful and does not harm plants, so well suited for an already planted community tank containing tank-mates which are not too big. Accepts dry food, but also needs live food occasionally. Place several in large tanks (25-gallon capacity and up). The males circle each other, croaking, but these encounters are harmless. This species should be made more available commercially.

**Breeding**: Breed in pairs in planted tanks measuring 20 inches or more along a side. Include floating plants (water sprite). Breeding of well nourished fish is easy. A flowerpot-cave serves as a nest-building site, although the nest is often built at the surface of the water, under floating plant leaves.

You can often see the female's tranquilizing maneuvers at the beginning of the spawning phase: in a horizontal position, she turns over on her side and presents her belly to the male. Then she stimulates her partner by wave-like blows with the hind part of her body or her tail. This movement presses him into the side of the female, who is now broadside to him, and he embraces (wraps himself around) her, turning her over on her back. In two or three seconds a white egg clump or packet appears and begins to fall toward the bottom. The male immediately snaps up the egg clump and carries it to the nest. Normally, about 200 eggs, exceptionally up to 500 eggs, are produced every spawning phase.

After the spawning phase, remove the female from the small breeding tank. In larger tanks she can indirectly care for the brood by defending the territorial periphery.

The young hatch in one and a half days, at which time the father

usually moves his nest to the surface of the water, if it was in a cave before. The young swim free in about four days following laying of the eggs, and need freshly hatched *Artemia* nauplii for their first food.

Growth is uninterrupted.

*Note*: The fish – males and females both—produce clearly audible croaking sounds during their hierarchical fights and courtship rituals.

In northeastern Malaya, where *Betta splendens* and *Betta imbellis* are absent, the croaking gouramis are called "fighting fish" and also used in fish fights like the *Betta*.

## Addenda

### ADDENDA

As this book went to press, several new species were described, and a new observation was recorded with *Betta coccina.*
Rather than leave this book without two new species, I convinced the publisher to put in this addenda.

*Parosphromenus harveyi* in a spawning embrace in their cave. Photo by the author.

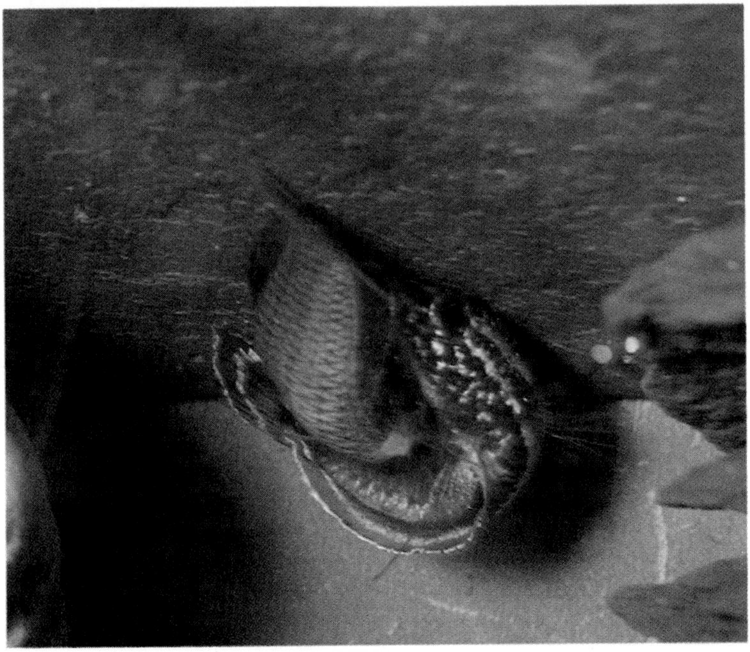

*Parosphromenus harveyi*, a species described in 1987. This pair was photographed by the author.

## *Parosphromenus harveyi* Brown, 1987

**Systematics:** First described in *Aquarist and Pondkeeper*, p. 34. An extremely poor description, but valid.

*harveyi*: Named for an English fish-breeder.

**Description:** Similar to *P. deissneri*. With cream-white body color and dark horizontal bars. The males have a characteristic dark spotted throat.

**Distribution:** Collected on the west side of Peninsular Malaysia near Batu Arang, in a pond near the street. Water tea-colored and clear, 28°C. Other fishes at the type locality: *Luciocephalus pulcher, Sphaerichthys osphromenoides, Betta coccina.*

**Maintenance and Breeding:** The same as for *P. filamentosus.*

## *Betta persephone* Schaller, 1986

**Systematics:** Originally described in *DATZ*, pp. 297-300. *persephone*: from Greek mythology; Persephone was the daughter of Demeter and Zeus.
**Description:** Closely related to *Betta coccina*, but the original description does not give differentiating characters. According to the original description it should remain somewhat smaller than *coccina*. Males in spawning coloration are dark, especially in their posterior half. Anal and dorsal fins as well as the scales in the posterior half of the body with beautiful green reflections.
**Distribution:** Southern part of the Malay Peninsula. *Locus typicus* is a pond about three kilometers north of Ayer Hitam. These fish like to hide among leaves.
**Maintenance:** The same conditions as for *Betta coccina*.
**Breeding:** Bubblenest builders that prefer caves. But they build only very small nests. It is not very difficult to breed, but it needs soft and acid water. Only about 100 eggs are laid.

*Betta persephone,* a species described in 1986. The male is shown here in his dark, breeding color phase. Photo by the author.

*Betta coccina*, a male from Sarawak. This geographical variety sports a much larger purple spot on its side than the original fish described from Sumatra. Photo by the author.

New information concerning *Betta coccina*: This species is also found in Borneo (Sarawak). The males of this population have a large greenish blue spot on each side larger than those found in *coccina* from Sumatra.

## *Parosphromenus allani* Brown, 1987

**Systematics:** Originally described in *Aquarist and Pondkeeper*, p. 34. A very poor description, but apparently valid.
*allani*: Named for Allan Brown.

**Description:** Similar to *P. deissneri*. With rose red body color and dark horizontal bars. The male's dorsal and anal fins each display a horizontal blue band that distinguishes them from *P. deissneri*.
**Distribution:** Caught in the outskirts of Sibu (Sarawak, Borneo) in a roadside pool. Water was tea-colored and clear, pH 5.4, dH 0.5, temperature 28°-34°C. Other fishes at the type locality: *Luciocephalus pulcher, Trichogaster trichopterus,* and *Rasbora* and *Barbus* species.
**Maintenance:** The same as for the other *Parosphromenus* species.

**Gouramis and Other Anabantoids**
**By Hans-Joachim Richter**
ISBN 0-86622-941-8
PS-874

*GOURAMIS AND OTHER ANABANTOIDS* is a completely up-to-date book on the subject of those aquarium favorites which breathe air and have magnificent color and diverse breeding habits, Most of the gouramis and anabantoids are either bubble-nest builders or mouth-brooders. The author is considered the world's greatest fish photographer. He is also an outstanding fish breeder and has bred species that no one else has ever spawned. His first breeding of the Chocolate Gourami, *Sphaerichthys osphromenoides*, proved with crystal-clear color photographs, established him as an authority on gouramis and related fishes and made his name known in all aquarium circles.

*6¼ x 9¼, 224 pages, library bound hardcover*
*Fully indexed; contains 323 full-color photos and drawings*

**BETTAS: A Complete Introduction**
**By Walt Maurus**
ISBN 0-86622-254-5
CO-005 Hardcover
ISBN 0-86622-254-5
CO-005S Softcover
ISBN 0-86622-288-X

Easy to read and loaded with practical, easy-to-apply information and solidly sensible advice, this highly colorful book covers every topic of importance to anyone—especially a beginner—interested in keeping *Betta splendens*, the Siamese fighting fish. Vital information is provided about the different types of bettas and what they need in order to live well: how to house and feed them, how to breed them, how to keep them healthy.

*5½ X 8½, completely illustrated with 110 full color photos and drawings.*

**FISH DISEASES: A Complete Introduction**
**By Dr. Gottfried Schubert**
CO-016 Hardcover
ISBN 0-86622-265-0
CO-016 Softcover
ISBN 0-86622-297-9

Anyone keeping an aquarium will sooner or later be faced with a sick fish. Teaching aquarists how to identify, treat and cure fish diseases is the purpose of this book. It is magnificently illustrated with full-color photographs and drawings and has been written by one of the world's leading fish pathologists.

*5½ x 8½, 96 pages*
*Contains over 100 full-color photos.*

# WEIGHTS & MEASURES

## CUSTOMARY U.S. MEASURES AND EQUIVALENTS / METRIC MEASURES AND EQUIVALENTS

### LENGTH

| | | |
|---|---|---|
| 1 inch (in) | | = 2.54 cm |
| 1 foot (ft) | = 12 in | = .3048 m |
| 1 yard (yd) | = 3 ft | = .9144 m |
| 1 mile (mi) | = 1760 yd | = 1.6093 km |
| 1 nautical mile | = 1.152 mi | = 1.853 km |

| | | |
|---|---|---|
| 1 millimeter (mm) | | = .0394 in |
| 1 centimeter (cm) | = 10 mm | = .3937 in |
| 1 meter (m) | = 1000 mm | = 1.0936 yd |
| 1 kilometer (km) | = 1000 m | = .6214 mi |

### AREA

| | | |
|---|---|---|
| 1 square inch ($in^2$) | | = 6.4516 $cm^2$ |
| 1 square foot ($ft^2$) | = 144 $in^2$ | = .093 $m^2$ |
| 1 square yard ($yd^2$) | = 9 $ft^2$ | = .8361 $m^2$ |
| 1 acre | = 4840 $yd^2$ | = 4046.86 $m^2$ |
| 1 square mile ($mi^2$) | = 640 acre | = 2.59 $km^2$ |

| | | |
|---|---|---|
| 1 sq centimeter ($cm^2$) | = 100 $mm^2$ | = .155 $in^2$ |
| 1 sq meter ($m^2$) | = 10,000 $cm^2$ | = 1.196 $yd^2$ |
| 1 hectare (ha) | = 10,000 $m^2$ | = 2.4711 acres |
| 1 sq kilometer ($km^2$) | = 100 ha | = .3861 $mi^2$ |

### WEIGHT

| | | |
|---|---|---|
| 1 ounce (oz) | = 437.5 grains | = 28.35 g |
| 1 pound (lb) | = 16 oz | = .4536 kg |
| 1 short ton | = 2000 lb | = .9072 t |
| 1 long ton | = 2240 lb | = 1.0161 t |

| | | |
|---|---|---|
| 1 milligram (mg) | | = .0154 grain |
| 1 gram (g) | = 1000 mg | = .0353 oz |
| 1 kilogram (kg) | = 1000 g | = 2.2046 lb |
| 1 tonne (t) | = 1000 kg | = 1.1023 short tons |
| 1 tonne | | = .9842 long ton |

### VOLUME

| | | |
|---|---|---|
| 1 cubic inch ($in^3$) | | = 16.387 $cm^3$ |
| 1 cubic foot ($ft^3$) | = 1728 $in^3$ | = .028 $m^3$ |
| 1 cubic yard ($yd^3$) | = 27 $ft^3$ | = .7646 $m^3$ |
| 1 fluid ounce (fl oz) | | = 2.957 cl |
| 1 liquid pint (pt) | = 16 fl oz | = .4732 l |
| 1 liquid quart (qt) | = 2 pt | = .946 l |
| 1 gallon (gal) | = 4 qt | = 3.7853 l |
| 1 dry pint | | = .5506 l |
| 1 bushel (bu) | = 64 dry pt | = 35.2381 l |

| | | |
|---|---|---|
| 1 cubic centimeter ($cm^3$) | | = .061 $in^3$ |
| 1 cubic decimeter ($dm^3$) | = 1000 $cm^3$ | = .353 $ft^3$ |
| 1 cubic meter ($m^3$) | = 1000 $dm^3$ | = 1.3079 $yd^3$ |
| 1 liter (l) | = 1 $dm^3$ | = .2642 gal |
| 1 hectoliter (hl) | = 100 l | = 2.8378 bu |

### TEMPERATURE

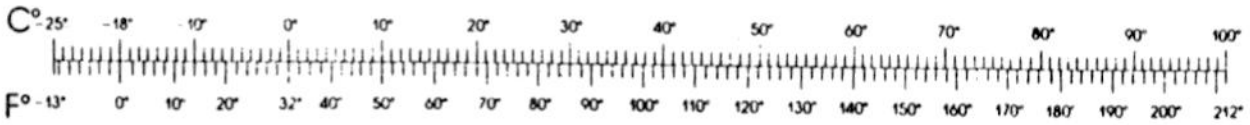


CELCIUS° = 5/9 (F° −32°) FAHRENHEIT° = 9/5 C° +32°

W9-BDW-006